Gender and Sexuality in the Classroom

Create a more gender-inclusive climate in your classroom and school. This important book breaks down issues of gender and sexuality at the individual, interactional, and institutional level and shows how you can cultivate an atmosphere of acceptance and belonging for all students.

You'll learn key concepts and terms educators need to know to support students, how gender and sexuality identities develop and influence mental health, why we should take an intersectional approach with students, and the importance of creating psychological safety in the classroom. You'll also gain practical suggestions on how to disrupt unconscious bias, represent diverse voices, counteract microaggressions, use gender-neutral language and preferred pronouns, address gender bullying, provide safe zones, and craft inclusive school statements. Each chapter contains examples, anecdotes from teachers and students, best practices, and resources to help you along the way.

Appropriate for educators of all grade levels, this book's clear, helpful advice will help you ensure that your students feel visible, affirmed, and safe, so they can thrive in school and beyond.

Marni Brown (she/her) is an associate professor of sociology at Georgia Gwinnett College and the Chair of Faculty for the Human Development and Aging Services program. In addition to these roles, she serves as the faculty advisor to the student group, Faces of Gender and Sexuality (FOGS).

Baker A. Rogers (they/them or she/her) is an associate professor of sociology at Georgia Southern University. Their research focuses on inequality, specifically examining the intersections of gender, sexuality, and religion in the U.S. South.

Martha Caldwell (she/her) consults and conducts workshops through iChange Collaborative. She has facilitated hundreds of conversations about race, gender, and social class experience with thousands of students, parents, educators, business professionals, and community leaders.

Also Available from Routledge Eye On Education
www.routledge.com/k-12

Let's Get Real, Second Edition: Exploring Race, Class, and Gender Identities in the Classroom
Martha Caldwell and Oman Frame

Facilitating Conversations About Race in the Classroom
Danielle Stewart, Martha Caldwell, Dietra Hawkins

Gender and Sexuality in the Classroom

An Educator's Guide

Marni Brown, Baker A. Rogers, and Martha Caldwell

NEW YORK AND LONDON

Cover image: © Alex J. Mack

First published 2022
by Routledge
605 Third Avenue, New York, NY 10158

and by Routledge
4 Park Square, Milton Park, Abingdon, Oxon, OX14 4RN

Routledge is an imprint of the Taylor & Francis Group, an informa business

© 2022 Marni Brown, Baker A. Rogers, and Martha Caldwell

The right of Marni Brown, Baker A. Rogers, and Martha Caldwell to be identified as authors of this work has been asserted in accordance with sections 77 and 78 of the Copyright, Designs and Patents Act 1988.

All rights reserved. No part of this book may be reprinted or reproduced or utilised in any form or by any electronic, mechanical, or other means, now known or hereafter invented, including photocopying and recording, or in any information storage or retrieval system, without permission in writing from the publishers.

Trademark notice: Product or corporate names may be trademarks or registered trademarks, and are used only for identification and explanation without intent to infringe.

Library of Congress Cataloging-in-Publication Data
A catalog record for this title has been requested

ISBN: 978-0-367-64583-0 (hbk)
ISBN: 978-0-367-63462-9 (pbk)
ISBN: 978-1-003-12531-0 (ebk)

DOI: 10.4324/9781003125310

Typeset in Palatino
by codeMantra

This book is dedicated to the remarkable teachers who strive every day to create inclusive classrooms, spaces that inspire growth and understanding in their students.

This book is also dedicated to the brave students, the change-makers who are leading us into the future of gender. We learn from you every day and remain in awe of your courage. Lead the way and we will follow.

Contents

Meet the Authors x
Acknowledgements xii
Preface: Introducing Ourselves: Why We Are Writing this Book xiii

Introduction: Gender and Sexuality in the Classroom: An Educator's Guide 1

1 **Individual Experiences of Gender and Sexuality** 23

2 **Disrupting Unconscious Gender Bias and Microaggressions** 43

3 **Interactional Experiences of Gender and Sexuality in the Classroom and Schools** 62

4 **The Application of Gender-Aware Critical Pedagogy** 89

5 **Institutional Experiences of Gender and Sexuality: Policies, Programs, and Plans** 110

Conclusion: Looking Forward 138

Glossary of Key Terms 144
Recommended Resources for Educators 151
Study Guide 160
References 162

Meet the Authors

Marni Brown (she/her) is an associate professor of sociology at Georgia Gwinnett College and the Chair of Faculty for the Human Services program. In addition to this role, she has served two terms as faculty senate vice president and the faculty advisor to the student group, Faces of Gender and Sexuality (FOGS). Marni has also been in the faculty affiliate to the Office of Diversity of Equity and Compliance at GGC. Marni has served as president for the Sociologist for Women in Society (south) professional sociological organization and has been elected as vice president to the Southern Sociological Society (SSS; 2023). She has published two anthologies (Sage Publications; Cognella Publishers), peer-reviewed articles (Teaching Sociology; General Anthropology), and has co-edited a special journal issue titled "Disability in the Wake of Covid" in the peer-reviewed, open-access journal SOCICATION. Marni lives in Atlanta with her wife, two kids, four dogs, and two cats.

Baker A. Rogers (they/them or she/her) is an associate professor of sociology at Georgia Southern University. Their research focuses on inequality, specifically examining the intersections of gender, sexuality, and religion in the U.S. South. Their books, *Conditionally Accepted: Christians' Perspectives on Sexuality and Gay and Lesbian Civil Rights* (Rutgers University Press); *Trans Men in the South: Becoming Men* (Lexington Books); and *King of Hearts: Drag Kings in the American South* (Rutgers University Press), can be found online. They co-edited a forthcoming volume of *Advances in Gender Research: Advances in Trans Studies* (Emerald Group Publishing). Their work is also published in numerous academic journals, including *Men and*

Masculinities; Journal of Interpersonal Violence; Gender & Society; and *Qualitative Sociology*. They serve as the President for Sociologists for Women in Society-South and serve on several committees related to diversity, equity, and inclusion. Baker lives in Columbia, South Carolina, with their wife, daughter, and two dogs.

Martha Caldwell (she/her) draws on the power of story to make the psychological dimensions of social identities visible. She has facilitated hundreds of conversations about race, gender, and social class experience with thousands of students, parents, educators, business professionals, and community leaders. The results enhance empathy, inspire innovative thinking, and catalyze leadership development. Her interactive, inquiry-based teaching style draws on 28 years of classroom experience that incorporates elements of social emotional learning, identity formation theory, and ethics. Martha consults and conducts workshops through iChange Collaborative and writes about identity equity in education. Her articles have appeared in *Independent Schools Magazine, Greater Good Magazine, Youth Today, Middle School Journal,* and *EdWeek*. She is co-author of *Let's Get Real: Exploring Race, Class, and Gender Identities in the Classroom* 2nd edition (Routledge) and *Facilitating Conversations about Race in the Classroom* (Routledge).

Acknowledgements

Alex J. Mack, a graduate of Georgia Gwinnett College, created many of the infographics for this book in addition to reading early drafts and providing feedback. Thank you.

Kaleigh Burch, also a graduate of Georgia Gwinnett College, read earlier drafts, provided feedback, and offered support. We appreciate the assistance. Thank you.

Preface

Introducing Ourselves: Why We Are Writing this Book

This book is for teachers who want to change the face of education, who want to create inclusive classrooms and schools in which our children can learn and thrive and grow. As the authors of this book, we each bring our own motivations and passions to this project, and together we bring the sum of our lived experience and professional expertise. We begin with a brief introduction of the authors.

Marni: What motivates me to write this book is my own membership in the gay community, my positionality as an educator, and my commitment as a parent of two young children who attend gender-affirming schools. I identify as a cisgender lesbian. I am white, Jewish, and a third-generation college student. My brother, a cisgender gay man, and I were both welcomed and accepted by our parents and family upon coming out. My path to being a lesbian, which included a lot of support and education, helped me develop a positive gay identity. Don't get me wrong, it was difficult at times. In fact, I struggled with what it meant to be a woman and lesbian in a heteronormative society; my reflection was difficult to find. But I knew it was out there. In fact, I landed in graduate school, studying gender and sexuality to better understand myself.

I have a graduate certificate in Women and Gender Studies along with a PhD in Sociology that focused on gender and intersectionality. I began my collegiate teaching career with classes on the sociology of gender and sexuality. I continue to teach these courses, not only to undergraduate students but also to faculty and staff via workshops and conferences. I work at a four-year, all-access regional college with primarily first-generation college students. At this institution, I am the faculty advisor to the student group Faces of Gender and Sexuality (FOGS) and co-coordinate an annual conference called "Intersections: An Interdisciplinary Conference for Gender and Sexuality." This conference allows students and faculty to present papers, projects, and research that speak to issues of gender and sexuality. My teaching, campus and community outreach, as well as research (which focuses on gender and sexuality) position me to work well with other educators.

Baker: What motivates me to write this book is my own positionality as a queer person, an educator, and a parent (of a toddler who I hope will have an inclusive education one day). I identify as a white, genderqueer, transmasculine, lesbian. I am an Associate Professor of Sociology at Georgia Southern University. I hold a PhD in Sociology, with a certificate in Gender Studies, and a Master's of Social Work. In addition to teaching sociology courses, I teach social services courses and womens, gender, and sexuality studies (WGSS) courses. My passion for social justice and activism leads me to teach with the goal of bringing about positive change and justice. Other identities I find relevant to this project include being a first-generation college student from a working-class background in the rural South. Because of my background, I did not have many resources or assistance in developing my gender and sexual identities. I desire to teach educators how to help gender and sexual minorities thrive in all educational settings.

With this specific project, I hope to provide educators with resources to help them understand gender and sexuality more fully. My desire is that educators will use this knowledge to provide safe and productive environments for all students to learn and grow, regardless of gender and sexuality. Using my own (often negative) experiences in education, as well as considering my students' stories and experiences, allows me to help educators realize the many areas where gender and sexuality are relevant in education. Additionally, my academic work and publishing focuses on gender and sexuality. Specifically, my research examines the intersections of gender, sexuality, and religion in the Southeastern United States.

Martha: I came of age as a cisgender, heterosexual, white woman in the 1960s during the Civil Rights Movement. My own awakening as a feminist and the "undoing" of internalized limitations in my own consciousness has been a life-long journey. As a mother and grandmother, I've watched three generations come of age. I've devoted my life to race and gender justice. As a classroom teacher, I developed curricula that facilitate healthy identity development. My method uses storytelling to launch inquiries into identity. Year after year, I listened to the stories my students told. Year after year, the faces changed, but the stories stayed the same. I saw young women struggle to hold onto their confidence as media images flashed before their eyes. I saw young men face ridicule if they spoke from their hearts. I saw gender nonconforming students grapple with transphobia and homophobia from peers and adults alike. For the past decade, I've worked as a diversity, equity, and inclusion consultant. Through iChange Collaborative, I work with a diverse group of professionals to help K-12 educators develop best practices to support healthy social identity development.

Overall, the three of us make a good team. Based on our unique backgrounds in the queer community, intersectional feminism, K-12 schools, and higher education, we are positioned to provide a unique perspective for K-12 educators that can be used in their classrooms.

A strict code of binary gender limits everyone's capacity for expression. Until these norms are relaxed, our children's potential for creativity, integrity, and joy will be limited. We believe educators are the world's best hope for change. There is no more caring and dedicated community of professionals. Because you are reading this book, it's likely that you, too, are inspired by your passion for equity and inclusion in education. We hope this book helps you develop your practice.

Introduction

Gender and Sexuality in the Classroom: An Educator's Guide

Gender and *sexuality* shape all areas of our lives, from the clothes we put on when we wake up in the morning to the laws that govern our world. Issues of gender and sexuality begin in early childhood and continue throughout a person's life. The first question we ask when we find out about the birth of a child is, "Is it a boy or a girl?" By the time children reach the age of one, they understand how to categorize people by gender (Pastel et al. 2019). By a year and a half, they start to understand their own gender, and by two years old, they can communicate this understanding, as well as gender stereotypes, to others (Pastel et al. 2019). By the age of six, they are aware of power differentials between men and women (Martin and Rubie 2010). In terms of sexuality, children begin to explore their sexual identity in early adolescence, around the ages of 10–13 years (Kar, Choudhury, and Singh 2015). Children bring their concerns and questions about gender and sexuality to school. School is a social institution where children spend a large majority of their time and interact with both the formal and informal curriculum of schooling.

Educators' understanding of gender and sexuality is especially vital when working with students whose gender or sexual identities do not align with what their peers, parents, teachers, and society expect. Specifically, *lesbian, gay, bisexual, transgender*, and *queer* (LGBTQ) students feel less safe and affirmed at school, at least in comparison to those who identify as *cisgender*

DOI: 10.4324/9781003125310-1

or *heterosexual*. Therefore, "LGBT inclusion is a matter of keeping young people safe and well" (Dellenty 2019:41). On average, 42.5 percent of LGBTQ students report feeling unsafe because of their gender expressions, 37.4. percent because of their gender, and 59.1 percent because of their sexual identities (Kosciw et al. 2020).

But gender and sexuality don't only affect LGBTQ students; gender and sexuality affect all students (Caldwell and Frame 2022). The harmful impact of gendered expectations has been evidenced in various educational, psychological, and sociological research (Dellenty 2019; Kosciw et al. 2018, 2020; Pascoe 2007; Pastel et al. 2019; Sadker and Sadker 1994; Travers 2018). That is why it is also important to include cisgender and heterosexual identities when discussing the effects of gender and sexuality on children and young people.

For example, many young, cisgender women experience a drop in self-esteem during adolescence. As young women move through puberty, they often struggle with body image issues and self-objectification as they begin to see themselves through the eyes of a gendered and sexualized society. By high school, significantly fewer cisgender feminine young women sign up for advanced math, science, and technology classes than cisgender young men (Inclusive Stem Teaching Project 2022).

Cisgender boys are affected by gender too. In early grades, many boys act out hypermasculine stereotypes on the playground, exclude girls from sports and games, and call other boys "girly," "sissy," or "fag" to insult them (Katz 2000, 2013; Newsom 2015; Pascoe 2007). To "act like a girl" or "throw like a girl" is considered "unmanly" and beneath the dignity of a "real" boy. Boys also enjoy far less room for gender expression than girls, especially when it comes to what they wear. The strict policing of gender norms among boys limits their capacity for caring relationships and emotional connections (Katz 2000, 2013; Newsom 2015; Pascoe 2007).

Overall, creating a gender-inclusive climate can powerfully impact learning and school success for all students. Inclusive campuses and classrooms focus on creating a community of learners with a sense of belonging for all involved. When students are invalidated and fearful, they are not free to learn, and they cannot thrive. When they feel visible and affirmed, however, they are free to be engaged and successful in school. Inclusive education can be a powerful and influential force in all students' lives. Understanding how gender and sexuality shape our lives allows educators to provide students with power, agency, and an essential path to social mobility.

Schools as Gendered Institutions

FIGURE 0.1
Source: monkeybusinessimages

Schools, like all institutions, are *gendered institutions* (Wade and Feree 2019). What is a social institution? Simply put, a social institution is anything in our society that constrains how people behave through systems and structures designed to provide rules for social order. Examples of social institutions include family, media, governments, religions, cultures, and economic systems. Since social institutions enforce rules and constrain behavior, they transmit social norms that can help members of the institution organize their lives. For instance, the family as an institution is responsible for teaching appropriate behavior, including how one should behave when out in public.

However, while institutions are powerful social forces that impact norms and behaviors, institutions aren't static entities. They are always changing and morphing because institutions exist as products of individuals interacting with their social world, and thus they are malleable. An important aspect of institutions is that they are created by people. Therefore, while people may be constrained by social institutions, they also have the agency or ability to change social institutions.

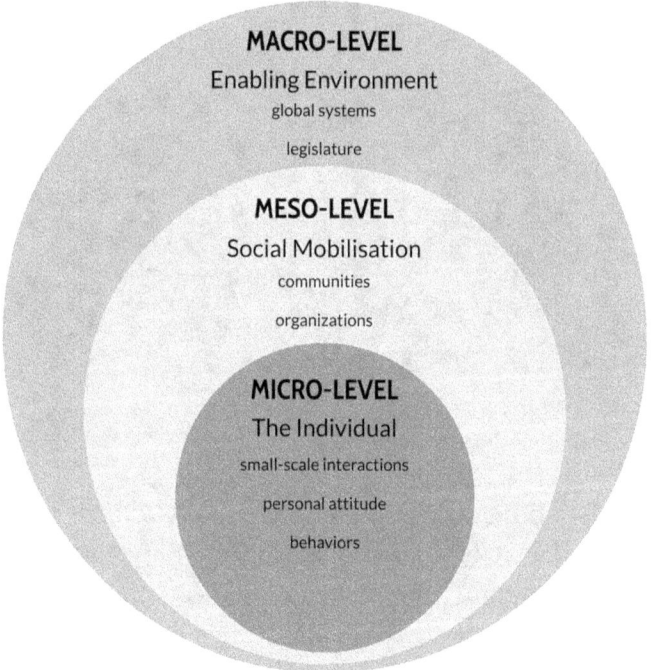

FIGURE 0.2
Source: Infographic by Alex J. Mack

An institution becomes gendered when both formal and informal policies make gender an important component to shaping how people behave. Within schools, education becomes gendered when teachers and administrators use gender as a dividing mechanism. Think about something as simple as what you ask your students to call you. Most teachers use honorifics such as "Ms." or "Mr." While this may seem like a small thing, it immediately tells students that gender matters, and most likely that gender is binary, meaning there are only two options—man and woman. (A few teachers are starting to use gender-neutral honorifics, such as "Mx.," which we will discuss in more detail later in this book.)

Another example of gender as an institution within schools is dress codes. If you teach at a school with dress codes or uniforms, most of these are still gender specific (Knipp and Stevenson 2021). Dress codes are often utilized to create order and limit what are perceived to be distractions; however, they are often cis- and heteronormative, imbalanced, and unequal. Most dress codes constrain girls more than boys and limit all students' gender expressions. For example, in some schools in Georgia, graduation gowns are even colored differently for girls and boys.

In addition to formal gender policies, schools are also informally gendered. For instance, sometimes teachers use gender to divide a class and even create "teams" for activities. Or they may unquestioningly consider playgrounds as visible spaces for the gender divide to occur (Martin 1998; West and Zimmerman 1987). While most of the time students aren't mandated to play in certain areas or play certain games on the playground, gender often becomes a dividing factor, even during this "free" time.

Some teachers believe it is "natural" that students divide themselves along gendered lines on the playground; however, we hope it will become clear as you read further that this gender divide is not essential or "natural." We believe gender is socially created, and this divide is the way children express the differences they have been taught. Children learn gender expectations, both in terms of *gender expressions* (the way a person dresses and presents themselves to others) and *gender identities* (the internal awareness of one's own gender), very early in their lives. These expectations are reinforced in most social settings, including the playground. Hence, *gender becomes an institution that limits children's behaviors.* For some children, this is perfectly fine because they are comfortable with the expectations that have been placed on them. Problems arise for other children when these expectations keep them from being themselves and from being accepted because of their gender expressions or identities. Therefore, as educators, we must be aware of the constraints we experience in society and how they get placed on students. We must allow all students to express their gender and sexuality in ways that make sense to them.

Throughout this book, we use social science data and lived-experience narratives to demonstrate how the social categories of gender and sexuality matter, largely because of the way society and dominant culture give meaning to them. We explore the social categories of gender and sexuality as factors associated with school success. School success can mean many different things, and we are interested in how a student's gender and sexual identities impact their ability to be seen, heard, and affirmed in the classroom, because we know that students who feel validated by teachers and have a sense of belonging among their peers have higher rates of school success.

There is clear research indicating that LGBTQ youth are significantly more vulnerable than their cisgender and heterosexual peers when it comes to mental health and school acceptance (HRC 2021; GLSEN 2021; Trevor Project 2021; Williams

Institute 2021). We want to help you create safe spaces for all students, regardless of their gender and sexuality. Therefore, our intent is for educators to make sense of students' classroom experiences through a gender and sexuality lens, bringing into focus the profound ways contemporary notions of gender and sexuality influence school-aged children. Many schools establish learning objectives for students to measure classroom success, and we believe learning standards should reflect and include social and cultural awareness, as well as empathy toward others. The ability for a student to succeed, both inside and outside of the classroom, is closely related to their ability to feel welcomed and affirmed, regardless of how they identify.

We understand that gender and sexuality can be intimidating topics. Many educators believe strongly in students' right to gender expression and want to help them strengthen their identities, but nonetheless, find themselves in the position of negotiating a political school environment based on traditional and/or religious beliefs. Many teachers, for good reasons, fear backlash for introducing important topics related to gender and sexuality that some people consider taboo. These concerns reflect a cultural history in which cisgender and heterosexual identities have been elevated and transgressing these binary categories has been considered socially unacceptable.

Despite political differences, we have never encountered an educator who did not believe that regardless of a student's gender or sexual identities, they have the right to learn in a safe and comfortable environment. Therefore, all educators, no matter where they fall along the political spectrum, must challenge themselves to continue learning, and most importantly, to listen with empathy to students so they can understand the challenges these students are facing in our classrooms and schools.

Language Matters: Terms and Definitions

To assist with the understanding of gender and sexuality, we provide definitions of key terms and concepts, as well as evidence-based practices for how to create gender and sexuality inclusive classrooms and schools. Developing a shared language to respectfully talk about gender and sexuality is an important starting point. The language we use to navigate our experiences with gender and sexuality is rapidly expanding, and new concepts and terms to describe categories of experience are entering the lexicon all the time. If you are new to the topics of gender and sexuality, you can reference the Glossary of Terms at the end of the book, but keep in mind that while these terms are the most up-to-date available at the time of this writing, some concepts may shift over time. For gender-inclusive educators, it's important to stay up-to-date on the evolving language.

Cultivating language is a generative process, so consider that we are not only learning the language but are also creating a new language in our conversations with students and colleagues. A good rule of thumb is to ask students about the identifiers they prefer *and what that means to them*. While we define these concepts, the meanings may also vary by individuals, cultural groups, and locations.

Finding, developing, and using language that aligns with what a person feels inside strengthens their identities. When educators honor students' preferred pronouns, they convey respect and validate their sense of self. For some students, discovering new vocabulary can be liberating. As Hunter, a nonbinary student says:

> I didn't know what nonbinary was until I heard someone use the word in a Tik Tok video. As soon as I found out what that word meant, I knew that was me. I'd always felt like there was no place I fit in, but suddenly I found out there were a lot of people like me.

Sex, Gender, and Sexuality

A lot of people use the terms *sex*, *gender*, and *sexuality* interchangeably, however, these are distinct concepts, and each of these aspects of an individual's identity falls along a continuum. *Sex* refers to the biological characteristics used to divide humans into categories, usually male and female. These biological characteristics include, but are not limited to genitalia/anatomy, hormones, and chromosomes. While sex is based on biology, it is also socially constructed, meaning that we, as a society, decided what characteristics make a male and what characteristics make a female and assign value and meaning to these sex characteristics. Important to note, these biological markers shift over time and do not always neatly align with the *binary sex system* of male and female. For instance, *intersexuality* encompasses an array of differences that do not fit neatly into one of these two categories.

Gender is related to sex but includes distinct characteristics that refer to the social expectations we place on people, usually based on their assumed sex category (West and Zimmerman 1987). Gender is an identity, a performance, and a social institution. It describes how a person performs masculinities and femininities in interaction with others, and how these performances are judged or policed by others. Before we are even born, everyone wants to know, "What's it going to be?" By this they mean, is the baby going to be a boy or a girl. Technicians who perform ultrasounds in OB-GYN offices or birth centers present the findings in a gender-binary format; some might even place the picture results in pink or blue envelopes. Based on this information, which is really about the fetus's biological sex, not their gender, society begins to place expectations on a child before they are born.

As soon as a child comes out of the womb, society and culture begin to socialize them into the expected behaviors and presentations thought to be appropriate for their sex. Little girls are taught to "act like a girl," and little boys are taught to "act like a boy." Gender is not something that comes naturally; rather, it is taught and practiced, rewarded, and then it is heavily policed and enforced by society. Why do some dads get mad when their son plays with a Barbie doll? Why do some moms freak out when their tomboyish little girl doesn't grow out of this "phase" quickly enough? Even if parents are accepting of their child's gender-expansive behavior, they may fear the consequences their children will face in society. As West and Zimmerman (1987, 2009) explain, whether people follow the rules of gender or not, they are always held accountable for acting in a way that aligns with the gender we assume they should be.

Sexuality refers to attraction and desire, both sexually and romantically, and isn't necessarily related to our assigned sex or assumed gender. People may have a variety of sexual and romantic attractions or interests, and these can change over time. The list of possible sexualities and combinations of sex/gender/sexuality is endless. A helpful way to distinguish between these categories is presented in Sam Killerman's "Genderbread Person" (The Genderbread Person, v. 4, 2018).

One of the most important things to remember when talking about gender and sexuality is that these are critical identities to all of us, even though the consequences of these identities impact gender-nonconforming individuals more severely. A cisgender person will have different experiences than a transgender person, but both will have experiences defined by their gender.

Finally, gender and sexuality are not binary categories, meaning that for the purpose of this book we are not only talking about girls/women and boys/men, or straight/gay when we use these terms. There is a wide and diverse range of genders and sexualities. Woman, man, trans, gender nonbinary, heterosexual, bisexual, gay, lesbian, queer, and asexual are some of the descriptors used for talking about gender and sexual diversity in our culture today.

The Genderbread Person v4

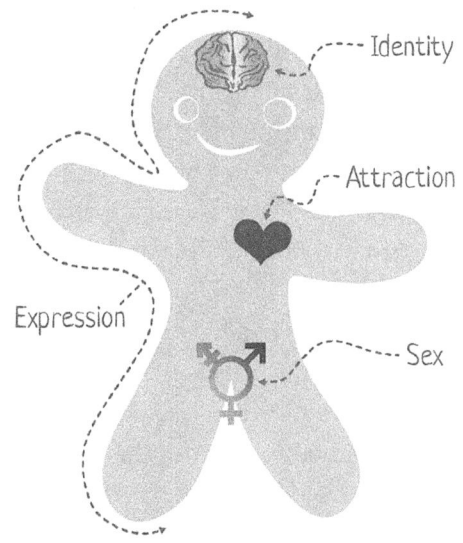

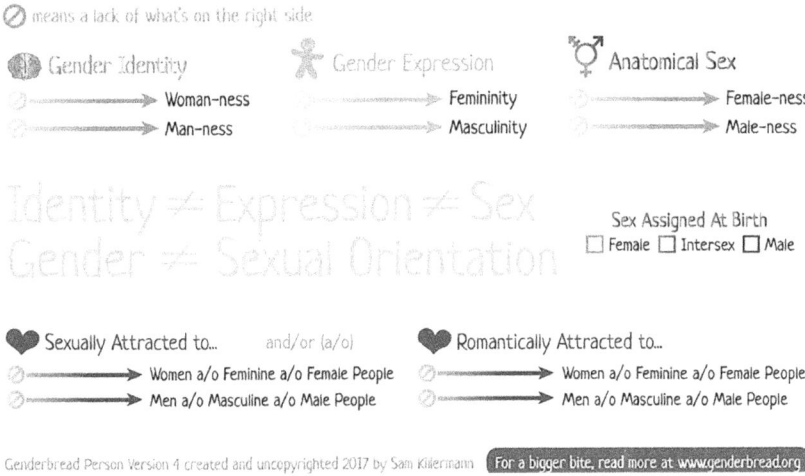

FIGURE 0.3
Source: Created and "uncopyrighted" by Sam Killermann

Transgender, Cisgender, and Nonbinary

Here are a few more specific terms that we use throughout the text. *Trans*, or *transgender*, refers to an individual whose gender identity does not align with the sex they were assigned at birth.

Trans is also used as an umbrella term, which includes a variety of identities, outside of the gender binary, such as genderqueer. *Cis*, or *cisgender*, in contrast, refers to a person whose gender identity aligns with the sex they were assigned at birth (i.e., a person assigned female at birth who identifies as a woman, or a person assigned male at birth who identifies as a man). Individuals who use gender nonbinary classifications tend to think of gender as a multidimensional spectrum, or continuum. *Nonbinary* people tend to fall outside the two primary positions of manhood/womanhood. Again, in a broader sense, nonbinary is an umbrella term for anyone who does not identify within the gender binary (Williams 2017).

Notice that while trans, like cis, is frequently used as an adjective to describe someone, it is not the whole of their identity. Therefore, as you never see "whiteman" or "gayman" written as single words, we also do not write transman or transwoman as single words. It is a good rule of thumb when speaking about identity to always include a person (i.e., trans man, not a trans; cis person, not a cis; lesbian woman, not a lesbian); to always use the identity as an adjective that is separated from the person with a space (gay man, not gayman); and not to add an "s" on identities (i.e., the gays; the transgenders; the asexuals). Think about it. No good sentence ever started with "The Blacks..." The same is true here regarding gender and sexuality.

Identity Formation and School

Let's start thinking about our own identities. Let's first consider your identity as a teacher and an educator. You've probably found that how you view yourself as a teacher is an ongoing process that changes over time. Your identity as a teacher is influenced by external factors, such as life experiences, job experiences, gender, race, sexuality, ethnicity, and religion (Flores and Day 2006; Rodgers and Scott 2008; Sachs 2005; Van Veen and Sleegers 2006; Zembylas 2003). You might feel like a good teacher one year (or one day), and a not-so-good teacher the next. You might think of yourself as an innovative teacher when you're young, but then feel stuck later in your career. Or you may feel yourself evolving over time and growing stronger with continuing professional education and experience. Why did you become an educator? Was it to become a special teacher or administrator like the one you admired in school? Was it your love of learning? Your desire to work with children?

In addition to your identity as an educator, you also all hold a variety of other identities that influence and intersect with your teacher identity. Maybe you identify as a Black man who is not only a teacher but also a parent. Or, maybe you identify as Hispanic, genderqueer, a teacher, and a hiker. Whatever the combination of characteristics and roles that make up your identity, these matter to who you are as an educator. As educators, our school experiences have had a large impact on our lives. In many ways, school plays a tremendous role in shaping our identities, and by understanding our own identity experiences, we are in a better position to understand our students.

Identity development theory, originally theorized by psychologist Erik Erikson (1968), proposes that a sense of identity enables people to move through life with purpose and direction. Identity allows us to feel a sense of inner sameness and continuity over time and place. Over the course of our lives, our identity is shaped by our individual, biological, and psychological capacities, in combination with the opportunities and support offered by our social contexts and environments. Identity development is a central issue for most during adolescence—when decisions about who we are, and our future vocational, ideological, and relational desires are addressed. However, for some individuals, identity work starts at a much younger age. And identity development is not something that one resolves or completes, rather identities continue to evolve and change over the course of our lives (Erikson 1950, 1968; Kroger 2007). Identity development is a lifelong process that demands reflection and revision throughout our life course.

It is our perspective that all identities are *socially constructed*, and thus evolve and develop in context and over time (Berger and Luckman 1964). Therefore, your teacher identity is not fixed or static, but rather shifts as you move into your profession and gain experience (Beauchamp and Thomas 2009). Social and cultural norms—what is thought to be socially and culturally standard or usual—are designed by society through agreed-upon interactions between people and passed on through observation and practice. Dominant culture influences the development of currently accepted social and cultural norms. As Olsen (2008) explains, we construct an internal sense of ourselves based on contextual interactions; as educators construct their identities, these constructions of self then become intertwined with the flow of activity in the classroom. Because of the importance of your teacher identity, Olsen (2008) claims that an examination of this identity can be used as a frame to examine aspects of teaching and connections with students.

The human development perspective (Freud 1920; Piaget 1972) argues that teachers and students have identities that are formed at the intersections of biology, psychology, and social forces. Human development work relies on the life span approach, which suggests that development is multidimensional and multidirectional. Human development also provides a complex framework for how one comes to understand and experience the world around them.

In schools, a human development perspective helps to explain some of the disparate outcomes based on gender and sexuality (Copur-Gencturk, Cimpian, Lubienski, and Thacker 2020). For illustration, while there is no average gender gap in math test scores when boys and girls enter kindergarten, a gap develops in favor of boys by around second or third grade (Copur-Gencturk et al. 2020). Something is happening between kindergarten (ages 5–6) and second to third grade (ages 8–10) that is critical to gender differentials in math skills. One explanation for this growing gap is that teachers, peer groups, and media begin to have a greater impact on shaping children's self-perception during this period. Around age five, when students begin school, girls generally have a strong sense of self. Yet, by the time girls reach ages eight to nine, they experience a significant drop in self-esteem (Gilligan 1982; Orenstein 2011). This does not happen to all girls, and there are now more opportunities for all genders to express themselves in ways that have not been available in the past, but this trend persists.

The range of gender expressions and identities now visible, especially because of social media, helps individuals see various ways they can engage in self-expression and identity (Wood, Bukowski, and Lis 2016). Yet, even with this progress, research shows that girls begin to become aware of how others see them (Gilligan 1982; Orenstein 2011, 2016) and at times cater to, consciously or unconsciously, the expectations of others. Additionally, girls begin to deal more with the male and heterosexual gaze, a social phenomenon closely related to the gender binary, which sexualizes them at young ages and creates unhealthy norms (Jean Kilbourne, Killing Us Softly).

One concept that helps us think about how our identities are influenced by those around us is sociologist George Herbert Cooley's (1902) idea of the "looking-glass-self."

FIGURE 0.4
Source: Bhupi

Furthermore, the looking-glass self refers to how people shape themselves based on other people's perceptions of them. So, if one is perceived as nice, then they will continue to do nice things to reinforce this positive perspective. Perception is greatly influenced by the dominant culture and can lead all students to reinforce gendered images of themselves to receive approval and praise from others (Goffman 1959). For instance, many boys feel the pressure to use their bodies in powerful ways and contain all their emotions except for anger, because they are taught this is what men are supposed to do (Newsom 2015; Porter 2010). Like all categories, placing boys and men in a limited box of what it means to be a man creates strict constraints for acceptance.

We call on educators to question, explore, and understand the impact of the education system on the vulnerable psyches and souls of the children and young people we interact with, especially regarding the binary construction of gender and sexuality. It is imperative for us to understand the impact on ourselves first so we can be present and attentive to the needs of our students. Our goal in this book is to help educators recognize the role gender and sexuality have played in shaping their own identities, their students' identities, and how these characteristics impact their classrooms and schools.

Intersectionality

Since the late 1980s, intersectionality has become a widely applied and innovative way of thinking about how all social structures and diverse identities shape individuals, communities, groups, and societies. Intersectionality refers to the interlocking nature of privilege and oppression in our society. This framework examines the intersections of race, gender, class, sexuality, ethnicity, immigration status, ability, etc. The concept of intersectionality was originally proposed to explain the ways race, class, and gender intersect for Black women in the United States (Collins 1990; Crenshaw 1989). While laws and policies existed to protect women from prejudice and discrimination, and other laws and policies existed to protect Black people from prejudice and discrimination, Black women often fell through the cracks and were not protected by either set of laws.

For this book, our interest lies in thinking about how the social categories of gender and sexuality shape opportunities for students in schools with their peers, teachers, and administrators. However, while gender and sexuality are our primary points of interest, it is vital to remember that these identities interact continuously with all of our other identities (Brown and Stewart 2018; Lewis 2003; Lewis and Diamond 2015). Considering this, scholar Jody Herman (2013) has documented the chronic stress transgender students face in schools, primarily when it comes to bathroom use. Herman argues that trans youth experience both verbal and physical harassment in both bathrooms and locker rooms. Yet, such discrimination is significantly higher for trans youth of color. Therefore, intersectionality reveals the complicated inequality youth experience at the intersections of marginalized gender, sexual, and racial identities.

In another example, Educator Monique Morris (2016) demonstrates that Black girls experience harsher punishment in schools than white girls, and many have spent most of their school years misunderstood and marginalized. Morris (2016), as well as others (Love 2019; Morris 2012), remind us that understanding and applying intersectionality is vital to the way gender and sexuality matter in our students' lives. Attention to intersectionality helps us promote a more diverse, inclusive, and equitable educational environment for all students.

Gender-Aware Critical Pedagogy

A gender-aware critical pedagogy begins with an educator's exploration of their own gender and sexual identities and calls for an examination of childhood conditioning and school experiences related to gender and sexuality. This self-knowledge is an important component in cultivating awareness of how students may be experiencing their gender and sexuality and enables educators to respond to children and young people with empathy and compassion. It cultivates consciousness of gender and sexuality as social institutions that influence us in ways we may not even be conscious of. It prepares us to challenge both the explicit and the hidden curriculum of schooling as it relates to gender and sexuality, and address it on both personal, interactional, and institutional levels.

Gender-aware critical pedagogy emphasizes the importance of recognizing, validating, affirming, and empowering students' identities. The teacher models these strategies and cultivates them in their students. This involves creating an identity-safe (and brave) learning community. When educators intentionally cultivate an atmosphere of respect and acceptance, the classroom becomes a place where students feel a sense of belonging and all students can thrive. Cultivating a safe and brave community involves teaching social-emotional skills in the context of gender equity and justice—skills that include listening with compassion, giving supportive feedback, and encouraging others. Such an approach involves teaching self-reflection, self-attunement, emotional literacy, and emotional regulation.

Gender-aware critical pedagogy also means representing gender-diverse voices and perspectives throughout the curriculum. It can mean reading stories or introducing texts with women and LGBTQ authors, characters, or themes. It can mean exploring history through a gender and sexuality lens. It can mean displaying posters with a diversity of gender and sexual identities on the walls of your classroom. It can mean providing opportunities for students to bring their lives outside of school into the classroom and share the ways their gender and sexual identities impact them as part of the curriculum.

Organization of the Book

The chapters of this book break down issues of gender and sexuality in education at the individual, interactional, and institutional levels. We have taken this approach because of the significance of gender and sexuality as social categories; categories that can order our lives individually, interactionally, and institutionally.

First, in Chapter 1 we examine how individual experiences of gender and sexuality influence identity development and educational success. Because school is a primary agent of socialization, we introduce concepts educators need to know to support students. In this chapter, we address the development of gender and sexual identity, explore the variety of identities within each category, and demonstrate why intersectionality matters when examining these identities. We discuss what educators should understand about the process of gender transitions. We describe the influence gender and sexual identities can have on mental health in youth, with specific attention to how mental health outcomes relate to how fully these identities are accepted. We include ways educators can ensure they are taking a gender affirmative approach.

In Chapter 2, we explore how to disrupt unconscious bias by looking at how teachers and administrators interact with students in the classroom and beyond. We explore how unconscious bias results in microaggressions (and sometimes *macro*aggressions) and can take the form of misgendering, deadnaming, not using a student's preferred pronouns, or asking invasive, personal questions. Because microaggressions are pervasive and recurring for students whose identities don't conform to traditional gender and sexuality norms, their effects are cumulative and take a mental and emotional toll. We stress the importance of cultivating self-awareness as an educator's first step in developing the capacity to recognize the ways unconscious bias manifests on personal, interactional, and institutional levels. Finally, we discuss how to counteract gender bias and microaggressions, how to respond appropriately to unintentional mistakes, and suggest activities to practice using gender-neutral pronouns.

Chapter 3 addresses the ways gender and sexuality intersect with both the hidden and formal curriculum of schools, recognizing that biased pedagogical strategies are pervasive in schools. We emphasize the importance of taking an intersectional approach to interactions with students and reemphasize the importance of using gender-neutral and inclusive language and honoring chosen names and preferred pronouns to affirm diverse identities. We discuss how unexamined teacher/student interactions may result in a self-fulfilling prophecy that reproduces and perpetuates gender inequality and how the phenomenon of stereotype threat plays out for women and girls in STEM subjects. We also address teacher identities and what is at stake for LGBTQ teachers and administrators. For example, Connell (2015) documents in her book, *Schools Out: Gay and Lesbian Teachers in the Classroom* that most LGBTQ teachers and allies are trying to strike a balance in the classroom that respects inclusivity but in the context of toxic and pervasive homophobia. For many teachers, creating a space that respects and honors gender and sexual diversity can be seen as risky, even political. Finally, we discuss approaches educators can use to support parents of students with diverse gender and sexual identities.

Chapter 4 explores gender-aware critical pedagogy. Following in the tradition of critical pedagogy, we draw on the work of Freire, hooks, and other theorists to build a framework for facilitating identity development and cultivating both a sense of agency and a sense of solidarity in students. We offer a framework for guiding inquiries into topics about gender and sexuality with students. Like other critical frameworks, gender-aware pedagogy centers students' lived experience, acknowledges learning as a communal process, and sees students as knowledge creators rather than knowledge consumers. Through a process of inquiry, students explore real-world problems with an eye toward social transformation. Because their lives are at the center of the curriculum, students are engaged in the process and inspired to learn. Because critical pedagogy is a method for surfacing unconscious assumptions and making implicit thinking visible, we emphasize the role of self-examination for educators who engage in a gender-aware pedagogical practice; the necessity of creating psychological safety in the classroom; the value of taking an intersectional approach in conversations about students' identities; and the importance of representing diverse voices and perspectives throughout the classroom and curriculum. We discuss the importance of curricula that are both emotionally and academically rigorous. We provide examples of methods and approaches educators are already using in their classrooms.

In Chapter 5, we discuss how education as a social institution can be more welcoming and inclusive to all students. This chapter takes an institutional view and discusses schooling as a primary institution of socialization; one that embeds a hierarchical gender binary in several ways. Schools regulate gender and sexual identity and expression through curriculum, dress codes, classroom activities, and access to extracurricular activities such as clubs and sports. We examine how policies, programs, and plans can support gender and sexual inclusivity in both the classroom and in the larger school setting. We explore controversies surrounding Title IX, sex education, bathroom access for transgender and nonbinary students, the importance of addressing gender bullying, and providing safe zones and affinity spaces for LGBTQ students. We look at diversity, equity, and inclusion statements, as well as plans, programs, and policies that have worked to support inclusivity and a sense of belonging. Throughout the chapter, we provide examples of teachers and schools who are responding with practices that make their entire schools more inclusive.

In the Conclusion, we offer a summary of best practices as discussed throughout the book. Many of these practices are evidenced in our work with gender and sexuality inclusive educators and based on what we have seen work well in classrooms and schools on individual, interactional, and institutional levels. We conclude with a look to the future. We are amid a cultural shift in which each successive generation is more embracing of diverse and fluid gender and sexual identities. This means teachers must be prepared to understand and respond to individual students and social changes. This is more important than ever to our children. As educators, it is up to us to lead the next generation and ensure that they are safe and loved along the way.

1

Individual Experiences of Gender and Sexuality

FIGURE 1.1
Source: fizkes

"Are you a boy or a girl?" Sam, a five-year-old student asks a fellow class member. Children usually ask questions about someone's gender identity out of genuine curiosity, and their questions can be answered directly and with helpful information. Such questions present teachable moments, opportunities to explain that there are more options than just "girl" or "boy" for gender identities, and sometimes you can't tell how a person feels about their gender identity just by looking at them.

Why do people need to know what gender someone is? Why does it matter if your student feels like a boy instead of a girl, or if they feel like neither or both? On the surface, it doesn't, and they don't. However, as members of a society, we all know that "gender is one of the fundamental ways in which the social life of human beings is organized" (Blakemore, Berenbaum, and Liben 2012:1). So, even if at an individual level we feel that someone's sex, gender, or sexuality should not be the concern of other people, it still shapes our lives and remains an important aspect of social order and organization; therefore, it exerts a profound influence on all of us. As Blakemore et al. (2012:1) argue, "Worldwide there are few factors that influence the lives people lead from birth to death as much as the person's sex or gender. Gender matters from the trivial to the most profound aspects of a human being's life." The sex we are assigned at birth leads to assumptions about our gender and sexuality. After that, everything is affected.

Consider, the doctor completes an ultrasound and tells you, "It's a girl!" Now, really all they know is that it looks like the fetus has a vagina, rather than a penis, but this doesn't stop all your friends from buying pink clothes and baby dolls, and in this way, sex is used to assign gender. The gender that is assigned will likely affect the name you choose, the toys the baby is given to play with, and the nursery décor. Where do you even buy gender-neutral clothes or toys? Do they even exist? Typically, clothes labeled boy are the default and considered neutral and safe for "either" gender, but in contemporary times, anything pink or purple is only for girls.

The influence of the sex you were assigned at birth continues into adulthood with research showing that once your daughter grows up, if she has a stereotypical woman's name, rather than what is interpreted as a man's name, then she will be much less likely to get a call back for an interview when she applies to jobs. If her name suggests that she is a Black woman, then the chances of a call back for a job interview are even lower. For instance, one study conducted by Bertrand and Mullainathan (2004) found that Brad (perceived to be a white man's name) got a call back 15.9 percent of the times when he applied for a job. On the other hand, Aisha (perceived to be a Black woman's name) who applied to the same jobs with the same qualifications only got a call back 2.2 percent of the times she applied for jobs (Fryer, Pager, and Spenkuch 2013).

With gender (and sexual identities) playing such an important role in our experiences and life chances it is important to understand how these identities develop over the life course. Furthermore, what should teachers know and do to encourage healthy development for their students? In the United States today, most children enter school or childcare at a young age. In 2016, only about 7 percent of dads and 27 percent of moms were stay-at-home parents (Pew Research Center 2018). This means that most children in the United States are cared for from an early age by someone outside their immediate family. Once children enter kindergarten, most of their care and socialization takes place within schools. Unfortunately, many children are subjected to constricted "gender learning" from an early age.

Often this constricted gender learning is done implicitly and through hidden curriculum that teachers may not even be consciously aware of. As Ehrensaft (2016:221) explains:

> As soon as a teacher asks all the girls to line up on the left side of the room and all the boys on the right, every child in the class has been taught an important gender lesson: there are only two choices, boy or girl, and you have to fit into one or the other, and it's the teacher's choice, not yours.

This teaches children that if they feel they do not fit in either of the expected lines, they are odd or different in some way.

Dividing your class by gender is a microaggression against students who do not feel comfortable in the group they are assumed to fit into.

Many educators have found creative ways to avoid some of the microaggressions that surround the gender binary. Hennesey and Bloomberg (2020) call on educators to use gender-inclusive language, instead of addressing children as "boys and girls" because these binary categories exclude some children. Ehrensaft (2016) suggests an alternative method to dividing the class, everyone with birthdays from January to June in one line and everyone with birthdays from July to December in the other. Pastel et al. (2019) also suggest grouping students in ways that do not divide them along their identities such as "Turn to your elbow partner" or "Everyone with green on their clothes may head outside." Of course, there are many other options as well, such as, everyone whose name starts with A–M on this side and everyone whose name starts with N–Z on this side. Besides providing learning exercises, these kinds of divisions do not ostracize children who do not "fit" into binary gender categories.

As social scientists, we believe that society has a strong influence on gender and sexual identity development. Therefore, as mentioned in the introduction, we take a social constructionist perspective (Berger and Luckman 1966) in our thinking about gender and sexuality development. A social constructionist approach includes the way dominant forces, such as patriarchy and heteronormativity, provide meaning to social categories, including gender and sexuality. Through this lens, gender and sexuality encompass powerful roles and statuses in both society and culture. At the same time, what gender and sexuality mean and the value they hold can change over time. For example, we have seen the role of breadwinner move across genders; it is not just for men. Who qualifies to be a parent and caregiver has also shifted with the growth of LGBTQ families.

We also acknowledge that society is not the only driving force; there are biological and psychological components to the development of our various identities. To consider gender and sexuality as performed and influencing one's sense of being, we honor the significant role these categories have on everyday lives, and thus as people, we have the ability, and agency, to challenge or reinforce the current gender order in society.

FIGURE 1.2
Source: FatCamera

One excellent study that demonstrates the social construction of gender is Messner's (2000) study of children's soccer. Messner demonstrates how parents, coaches, and children together construct stereotypical gender ideals within a space where gender could, or should, be irrelevant. As Blakemore et al. (2012:195) put it, "Social constructionists remind us of how frequently gender is socially constructed when there is no compelling reason for it to be."

Sex and Intersexuality

We briefly described the differences between sex, gender, and sexuality in the introduction. Now, we will explore these categories/identities further, before discussing why they matter in the classroom. Remember, sex is the biological characteristics (genitalia, hormones, chromosomes, gonads, and secondary sex characteristics) used to divide humans into categories, usually male and female. When a person is born with a body that does not fit neatly into one of these two categories, this is considered *intersexuality*.

There are over 40 variations of the human body that medical professionals consider to be intersexuality. Only a small percentage of these concern the external and visible genitalia; therefore, many intersex people do not know they are intersex until later in life. While about two percent of births in the United States are intersex babies, only a small percentage of these have visible genitals that a doctor may suggest needs unnecessary surgery (InterAct 2020). When an infant's body does not "fit" into one of the two socially constructed categories of sex, male or female, often doctors rush to surgery or other medical procedures to align the body with the definitions of one of the two sexes in our current binary system.

However, today, a growing and vocal group of intersex advocates are fighting for individuals' rights to control their own bodies. They argue that to operate or induce medical treatment on infants when they are healthy and do not need the treatment is unethical and should be stopped immediately. Paradoxically, intersex people must fight not to have the surgeries they do not want, while trans people often must fight to have the surgeries they do want. As we will discuss shortly, not all trans people have or want surgery, but the point is that intersex people are operated on against their will and often without them even knowing or being informed. Many intersex people find out later in life that their parents, with the advice of medical professionals, chose to allow surgeries to be performed before they understood or had a right to object.

One interesting statistic to help you think about intersexuality is that there are more babies born with an intersex condition each year than are born with red hair. So, if you know someone who has red hair, chances are you also know someone who is intersex.

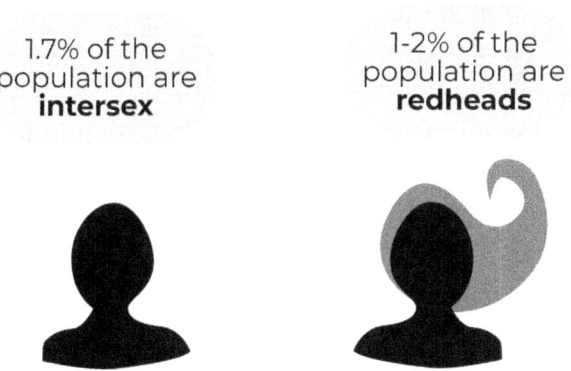

FIGURE 1.3
Source: Infographic by Alex J. Mack

Whatever the exact percentage of the population living with an intersex condition may be, you are likely teaching intersex students. They may know this, or they may not. They may know something is different about their bodies, or they may not. Either way, as equitable and inclusive educators, we should be sensitive to this topic and ensure that all our students feel safe and comfortable in our classrooms.

Gender Identity and Expression

Gender, as opposed to sex, refers to the distinct characteristics and social expectations society places on people, usually based on what their biological sex is assumed to be. Gender can be divided into at least two categories, *gender identity* and *gender expression*. Identity refers to how a person thinks about themselves. Do you think of yourself as a boy, a girl, a woman, a man, a trans person, a genderqueer person, a gender nonbinary person, or something else? Gender expression, sometimes thought of as performance, on the other hand, refers to how we demonstrate our gender to others. It is about how masculine, feminine, or androgynous we present ourselves. Gender expression can include clothes, makeup, accessories, and even how someone postures.

In your class, you may have students with a variety of gender identities, and their gender expressions may or may not align with their identities. *Cisgender* refers to people whose gender identity and performance align with the assumptions that have been made based on their assigned sex at birth. For example, if an infant is born with visibly male genitalia, then the doctor and parents usually assume that the infant is a male. Based on the sex category of male, society then makes several other assumptions, including the gender category of boy/masculine. We assume that males will grow up to be boys, then men, and that they will most likely be attracted to women when they are older. These are *cisnormative* and *heteronormative* assumptions. While most male children do grow up to be men and heterosexual, a lot of them do not.

Transgender students are those whose gender identity does not align with assumptions based on the assigned sex at birth. For instance, if a child's sex is assigned to be female, they may grow up to feel like a boy and man, rather than a girl and woman. Some people who are trans opt to take hormones that align with their gender identity or to have gender affirmation surgeries to align their biological sex more closely with their gender identity and expression, and other trans people choose not to take hormones or have surgeries and do not feel that sex and gender must align in assumed ways. The decision to alter one's body, or not, is made at the intersections of gender, sexuality, class, race, and social location. Sometimes medical intervention is not possible due to the costly and sometimes risky nature of such procedures.

Individual Experiences of Gender and Sexuality ♦ 31

FIGURE 1.4
Source: Infographic by Alex J. Mack

Gender nonbinary students may feel their identity falls in-between boys and girls, or that neither of these labels makes sense for how they feel about themselves. While nonbinary can stand alone as an identity, there are many other emerging identities that also do not conform to the gender binary such as *genderqueer, gender nonconforming, gender variant, gender fluid, gender creative, boi,* and *agender,* among others.

Halfway through the school year, Syd, an eighth-grade student in an urban independent school, began to share feelings of *body dysphoria* (the sense that his physical body did not match who he felt himself to be inside) with his fellow class members. He explained that his dysphoria began as a young child. Trying to fit into the role of a girl felt so forced to him that he struggled sometimes to get through the day at school. He was afraid that if anyone knew how he felt, he would become even more isolated. He couldn't concentrate on his schoolwork and his grades dropped.

Even though Syd's parents were not supportive at first, he never wavered in his conviction and was determined to live an authentic life. Over the course of the next two years, he changed his pronouns, his name, and his gender presentation. Ultimately realizing how crucial it was for their child's sense of well-being, his parents began to affirm his gender identity. Syd not only gained his family's support, but he had friends and a school community that stood behind him. As he developed a sense of being seen, he began to thrive. He became more outgoing and outspoken. His teachers began to see a passionate and vibrant student. He described feeling like someone had finally allowed him to be his whole self instead of only half. In high school, he mentored other trans and nonbinary students. Syd became one of the most respected young men at his school.

Syd's experience reflects the three key processes outlined by Johnson and Rogers (2020) that help mitigate the stress caused by the stigma and discrimination trans people experience: (1) normalization of trans identity and experience; (2) a social support system; and (3) opportunities for empowerment. Syd had a community that accepted him. They respected his decision to transition and honored his chosen name and affirmed pronouns. His parents were supportive and had the means to provide the gender affirming healthcare support and advocacy he needed. He was empowered with leadership opportunities in his school.

While Syd's transition was not easy, he had advantages that many trans children do not have. Many trans and nonbinary students remain invisible in our schools. They may lack support systems or families in a position to advocate for them. They may be afraid to come out because the threat of harassment and violence is very real. There would likely be many more stories like Syd's if it weren't for hostile school environments.

We are hearing from educators across the nation that they are seeing more and more children who identify outside of the binary categories of boy and girl. Because of this, Maria, an elementary school teacher, lets her students know that girls can have penises and boys can have vaginas and that gender identity does not depend on a person's body parts. Gender identity varies and depends on how a person feels about themselves and how they want to express themselves.

Gender Identity Development

Overall, there are three main approaches to understanding gender development: (1) biological, (2) socialization, or (3) cognitive (Blakemore et al. 2012). In this book, we take a socialization perspective to understanding gender development. While we acknowledge that biology (genes, chromosomes, hormones, etc.) influences physical functioning and behavior, and that cognition is important to how we think about and understand gender, from our perspective gender is most heavily influenced by society. Furthermore, because this book is meant for K-12 educators, the socialization approach will be important for you to understand as you consider the influence you and your teaching has on your students. More specifically within the socialization approach, we take a social constructionist view. Viewing gender as a social construction "proposes that knowledge can never be removed from social time and place" (Blakemore et al. 2012:16). The way we think about and perform gender is constructed, and these constructions influence how we act, think, and interact with one another.

Because gender looks very different across time and space, what it meant to be a girl when your grandmother was in elementary school is different from what it meant to be a girl when you were in school or from what it means for your students today. Furthermore, what it means to be a girl in school in the United States looks different than what it means to be a girl in school in Bulgaria or Afghanistan. These differences demonstrate that it is not biology that makes girls like certain things or act certain ways, rather, culture teaches us early what is appropriate for girls and boys in our society. Most modern societies leave it at those two binary options, although some societies do recognize third genders. For instance, before the white-settler colonization of native lands, in what is now the United States, many native tribes recognized third genders by a variety of names. Today, within some Native American and Indigenous cultures, the recognition of a third gender has reemerged and begun to be celebrated again. In some nations, this third gender is referred to as *two-spirit*.

In the United States today, adults are sometimes skeptical when children say they are not a boy or a girl in ways that align with society's assumptions. Nevertheless, research shows that for many children, gender identity development begins at a very early age. As mentioned in the introduction, by the age of one, children understand how to categorize people by gender, and by the age of two, they can understand and communicate their own gender (Pastel et al. 2019). By three, most children know some basic gender stereotypes and show preference for toys and activities associated with their gender (Blakemore et al. 2012). Therefore, by the time your students arrive in your classroom, most of them understand the importance of gender and have a sense of their own gender identity. This means the idea that "it's just a phase," or thinking that students do not understand gender is not sufficient. In fact, it can be harmful for working with students in the K-12 education system.

As Olsen et. al (2015) state, "Whether a child, who may or may not be transgender, is going through a phase is not really the point." Rather, the point is that a child needs supportive and non-judgmental adults to have their backs as they explore their gender identity and expression. Hence, "Letting a child know that they are loved and accepted unconditionally should always be the first course of action" (Olsen et al. 2015:251). Teachers do not need to be concerned with how the child will identify as an adult, or even next year; rather, they need to be respectful of the child's current identity and expression and provide a safe environment for them to continue exploring all their identities.

Ehrensaft (2016) labels children whose gender identity or expression does not match the sex they were assigned at birth, *gender creative* children. A gender-creative child "weaves together nature, nurture, and culture in an infinite variety of ways to establish the gender that is 'me'" (Ehrensaft 2016:7). Ehrensaft (2016:17) explains:

> I am neither an essentialist—one who says that gender is a given and set at birth or before—nor am I a social constructionist—one who says that gender is just a people-made concept that fluctuates over time. Rather, I am a transactionalist—one who says that nature and nurture crisscross over time in a myriad of ways in the context of each particular culture to create gender as we know it.

However you understand gender development, it is vital for teachers to adopt a "gender affirmative model" (Ehrensaft 2016). A gender affirmative model explains that gender variations are not some type of disorder; rather, they

> are healthy expressions of infinite possibilities of human gender; gender presentations are diverse and varied across cultures...; gender involves an interweaving of nature, nurture, and culture...; a person's gender may be binary... [or] fluid and multiple; if people suffer from any kind of emotional or psychiatric problem connected to their gender, it is most likely because of negative

reactions to them from the outside world; and if there is gender pathology, we will find it not in the child but in the culture.

(Ehrensaft 2016:15)

Children, and all people for that matter, are the experts on their own gender identities and expressions. While supporting gender variant children "can feel like a huge decision for most adults" (Olesen et al. 2015:252), once we accept that they are the experts of their own experiences, we can learn to listen better and help to translate what children are thinking and feeling.

Olsen et al. (2014) offer important points for adults to remember as they work with gender variant children. First, "Kids do the best they can with available vocabulary" (Olsen et al 2015:252). This means if we only give children binary language, it makes it more difficult for them to explain what they are feeling and need for adults to understand. Therefore, it is important for teachers to help all children learn language to explain a fuller range of identities than most of us were given as children. This goes along with Olsen et al.'s second point, which acknowledges that some children experience gender that is fluid and does not fit into the binary ideas society enforces. Third, gender identity and expression change over the life course for many people. Hence, "Gender, like life, can be a journey, not just a destination" (Olsen et al. 2015:252). This idea can be difficult for some adults to comprehend. A binary transition from boy to girl, or vice versa, provides some type of solution that may help adults wrap their heads around a child's gender. But, for some kids, there is no end point of transition, and as adults, our goal should be to normalize this variability, not try to create a solution. Finally, like all identities, gender exists in relation to our other identities and relation to others around us. While children will likely not put it in these terms, they are exploring and learning how their own identities fit together and how they fit in with those around them.

Social and Physical Gender Transitions

As teachers, you may work with some students who wish to transition their sex or gender socially or physically to better align with their gender identity. You can support students' transitions and provide parents with resources, such as gender literacy, for dealing with social and physical gender transitions. Socially, being cognizant of students' name preference and pronouns, even if this shifts multiple times over the course of a school year, is a small step that can make a world of difference to a gender variant child. Letting them know that you see them and that you respect them is the most important thing you can do as a teacher. Honoring students' chosen names and preferred pronouns conveys respect and validates their sense of self.

In 2020, the Trevor Project (2021) found that more than 50 percent of trans and nonbinary youth had seriously considered attempting suicide. Yet, the study also found that trans and nonbinary youth who had their chosen pronouns respected by important people in their lives attempted suicide at half the rates of youths who reported that their preferred pronouns were not respected. The survey revealed that two-thirds of LGBTQ youth live in homes that do not affirm their gender or sexual identities. Seventy percent said that they find affirming communities online, and 50 percent say that they find affirming spaces at school. Using students' chosen names and preferred pronouns empowers them with a sense of agency over their own experiences. *Dead naming*—refusing to call a trans or nonbinary person by their chosen name and insisting on calling them by the name that was assigned to them at birth—is a blatant reminder that they are not fully accepted by society (Rogers 2020). Thus, using chosen names and preferred pronouns is a way to model and teach how to demonstrate respect, acceptance, and affirmation. The Trevor Project's survey results clearly demonstrate the importance of affirming an individual's identities and being conscious of the language we use in the classroom and beyond. The case for educators creating gender-affirming spaces for these students is imperative. In short, it saves lives.

While physical and medical gender transitions are outside of your purview as an educator, it is important to be knowledgeable about these types of transitions for children and to know of appropriate resources to point parents to if necessary. Briefly, there are several medical interventions for gender variant children that may be appropriate based on the child's age. For K-12 educators, one of the most important medical interventions that you should be knowledgeable about are hormone or puberty blockers. Puberty blockers, given to children before the onset of puberty, suppress the child's development for a period. The benefit of this treatment is that it buys time for children and their families to decide what is the best option for the child. This gives the child more time to explore their gender identity and ensures that they are making the best decision for their future. Puberty blockers are fully reversible, meaning that they can be stopped, and puberty will progress as it would have without the blockers. However, if the child and family decide to move forward with gender transition, puberty blockers also "optimize the development of preferred physical characteristics" (Olson 2014:443). Specifically, blockers in trans girls stop the development of a deeper voice and penile enlargement, and in trans boys stop the development of breasts, hip widening, and starting menstruation. After the child has decided with their family how to proceed, they may then elect to have hormone replacement therapy (HRT) and/or gender affirmation surgeries to ensure that their bodies align with their gender identity.

Sexuality and Sexual Identity

Sexuality is about attraction and desire, both sexually and romantically, and isn't necessarily related to our assigned sex or our gender identity or expression. While sexual identity is often central in the lives of adolescents, "sexual feelings and romantic attraction arise sooner than many people may think" (Blakemore et al. 2012:6). Most children experience their first erotic attractions and feelings around age 10 and begin to explore their sexual identity in early adolescence around the ages of 10–13 years (Blakemore et al. 2012; Kar, Choudhury, and Singh 2015). This means if you teach fifth grade or above (and some students start earlier than others), you are likely working with students who are exploring their sexual feelings and identities. Therefore, teachers must be educated about sexuality and sensitive to implicit bias and assumptions about students' sexuality.

As with gender identities, there are numerous sexual identities and new categories are emerging. Furthermore, everyone has their own meaning and understanding of the identity they feel aligns best with them. While we can provide some general definitions of various sexual identities, remember that these are individualized identities and changing rapidly in our society. Generally, *lesbian* refers to women who are attracted to other women. *Gay* refers to men who are attracted to other men. *Bisexual* refers to individuals who are attracted to "both" genders, men and women. *Pansexual* refers to individuals who are attracted to people regardless of gender or to all genders; this differs from bisexual because it acknowledges that there are more than two genders in our society. *Asexual* refers to an orientation in which someone feels little or no sexual attraction to others. *Queer* (literally means odd or outside of the norm) refers to an identity that does not align with typical categories of identity. Therefore, queer could mean a lot of different things to different people. Finally, *straight* or *heterosexual* refers to individuals attracted to the "opposite gender." These are just a few of the identities that your students may find reflective of their relationships with sexual and romantic attraction.

Mental Health and Suicidality Among LGBTQ Youth

FIGURE 1.5
Source: SB Arts Media

Trevor Project's 2020 National Survey on LGBTQ Youth Mental Health examined the experiences of over 40,000 LGBTQ youth ages 13–24 across the United States, making it the largest survey of LGBTQ youth mental health ever conducted. The Trevor Project (2020) found that one out of every three LGBTQ youth reported being physically threatened or harmed due to their LGBTQ identity. Sixty-one percent of trans and nonbinary youth reported being prevented or discouraged from using a bathroom that corresponds with their gender identity. Almost one-third of LGBTQ youth had experienced homelessness, been kicked out of their homes, or run away from home. These negative experiences resulted in mental health problems, and an alarming 40 percent of LGBTQ respondents seriously had considered attempting suicide in the past 12 months.

GLSEN (2020) is a national organization started by educators to "conduct extensive and original research to inform our evidence-based solutions for K-12 education." The GLSEN 2019 National School Climate Survey (Kosciw et al. 2020) includes information on LGBTQ middle and high school students' experiences and demonstrates why understanding gender and sexuality is paramount to the safety and well-being of all students. In 2019, GLSEN (2020) found that six out of every ten LGBTQ students reported feeling unsafe at school due to their sexuality and more than four in ten felt unsafe due to their gender expression or identity. This led to one-third of LGBTQ students missing at least one day of school in the previous month. LGBTQ students avoided school bathrooms and locker rooms because they felt unsafe or uncomfortable.

Students felt unsafe for a myriad of reasons. More than 75 percent of LGBTQ students heard the words "gay," "fag," or "dyke" used in a negative way often or frequently at school, and more than 90 percent reported that they find such language distressing. More than half of LGBTQ students heard negative remarks about gender expression often or frequently at school, and almost half heard negative remarks about trans people often or frequently. Often negative language and remarks came from students, but more than half also heard homophobic or transphobic remarks from school staff. Furthermore, school staff rarely intervened when they overheard others using homophobic and transphobic remarks. Moreover, the negative comments and language included sexist language which also affects cisgender girls in schools, with more than four out of five LGBTQ students hearing sexist remarks often or frequently at school.

The negative experiences in school did not stop at language, but also included harassment and assault of LGBTQ students. More than eight in ten LGBTQ students experienced harassment or assault at school, most often related to their sexuality or gender expression. Approximately a quarter of students reported being physically harassed at school because of their sexuality or gender expression, with one in seven students reporting physical assault in the past year. Most LGBTQ students experienced bullying, in school and online. And nearly six in ten LGBTQ students were sexually harassed at school in the past year.

Unfortunately, this is not a comprehensive list of all the prejudice and discrimination that LGBTQ students experienced at school. Not all students report gender or sexual harassment for fear of consequences. Clearly, school is not a safe place for many LGBTQ students in the United States. Not only are they facing prejudice and discrimination from other students, but all too often school staff fails to intervene. Our hope is that with more education on gender and sexuality, all school staff will feel prepared to intervene and stand up for LGBTQ students.

Because we know that LGBTQ students, who are not affirmed in their sexuality or gender identities, are at an increased risk of suicide, it is important for teachers and administrators to be aware of the research on suicide and on the lookout for signs that a student may be at risk. If a student expresses suicidal thoughts, even if they ask you to keep it confidential, it is your fiduciary duty to seek outside help from your school counselor or administration immediately.

Conclusion

Binary conceptions of gender and sexuality may create order in society, but the order they create manifests in social disparities. In schools, power inequities manifest in painful social hierarchies that mirror society. Our job as educators is to recognize, affirm, and empower a range of diverse gender and sexual identities and teach our students to do likewise. With a critical eye to the ways gender and sexuality issues play in the lives of our students, we can provide learning opportunities that help them develop critical awareness and respond with agency to the world they live in. In short, we want to empower them to transform the social systems they inhabit.

2

Disrupting Unconscious Gender Bias and Microaggressions

FIGURE 2.1
Source: monkeybusinessimages

Beverly Johnson, a cisgender kindergarten teacher, has just finished reading *I Love You, Mommy and Daddy* to her class. "We got to hear about Little Bear's adventures playing with his mommy and daddy," she says. "Now, I want each of you to use your crayons to draw a picture of your mommy, daddy, and you playing together." Tamara shyly walks up to Ms. Johnson's desk as all of the other students take out their crayons and begin to draw. "Ms. Johnson, I don't have a daddy, so what am I supposed to draw? I have two mommies; can I draw them?"

Beverly, realizing she had forgotten about Tamara's family structure, says,

> Of course, you can! I should have been clearer that families come in all shapes and sizes, not just mommies and daddies. You draw a picture of you and your two mommies and let me tell the class that they can draw their family however it looks. Thanks for pointing this out to me!

Beverly stands up and makes a correction to her original statement about the book. "Class, the book we read was about a child with a mommy and daddy, but all families don't look this way. Instead of asking you to draw a picture of you, your mommy, and your daddy, I should have said that I would like you to draw a picture of whoever takes care of you. For some of you, that is two mommies, for some that is one mommy, for other students that is a grandma and a grandpa. I want you to draw your family the way it looks to you, because families come in all shapes and sizes. Once you finish drawing, we can read another book about how all families look different." After the students finished their drawings, Beverly pulls out the book, *My Family, Your Family* and reads it to the class.

Even though Beverly tries to be mindful and inclusive of all her students, in this case, her implicit and unconscious bias got in the way. Unlike *explicit bias* (which reflects the attitudes or beliefs that one endorses at a conscious level), *implicit bias* results from subtle cognitive processes (conditioned attitudes and stereotypes) that operate at a level below conscious awareness and without intentional control. Beverly was so used to thinking of families in one way, a mother, father, and children, that she had unintentionally excluded Tamara's family when she asked her students to draw a picture of themselves with their mommies and daddies. Her implicit assumption was that's how families look, and it didn't occur to her at that moment that not all students come from these kinds of families.

Unconscious Bias

Unconscious, or implicit, bias is like an operating system programmed into our brains. It's part of our social conditioning. Unconscious bias is made up of assumptions and attitudes that operate below the level of consciousness. The effects of both conscious and unconscious bias impact every aspect of our life. Unconscious bias surrounding issues of gender and sexuality manifests in schools in a myriad of ways from segregated bathrooms, to forms that ask for the names of "mothers" and "fathers," to lower expectations for girls in STEM classes, discipline disparities for boys, and unchecked bullying and harassment of LGBTQ students.

Unconscious bias can be at work when we don't even realize it, and sometimes when we are doing our best to prevent it. Jennifer Eberhardt (2019), author of *Biased: Uncovering the Hidden Prejudice that Shapes What We See, Think, and Do*, says bias is "a kind of distorting lens that's a product of both the architecture of our brain and the disparities in our society." Bias clouds perceptions, and because it interferes with one's capacity to see the full picture, it limits the capacity for good decision-making and interferes with the capacity for innovation.

For example, if we are unconscious that the leadership of most schools continues to reflect a gendered hierarchy (with most administrative positions filled by men while the vast majority of the teachers who report to them are women), we fail to fully recognize and leverage the talent women and gender-nonconforming people have to offer. The good news is that bias can be addressed appropriately when we become conscious of it. Research shows how we can shift previously held biases and counteract their negative effects.

Microaggressions

Unconscious, or implicit, bias often results in *microaggressions*—"subtle, verbal or nonverbal, insults directed toward people based on their belonging to a marginalized group," such as people of color, members of the LGBTQ community, people with disabilities, women, etc. (Sue 2010). These exclusions or subtle insults are often made automatically. Microaggressions include everyday slights, putdowns, insults, and sometimes even compliments that undermine a person's sense of identity and confidence. Microaggressions can be unintentional and are sometimes even well meaning, but their frequency over time has a cumulative impact. While these seemingly minor incidents of prejudice can appear to be harmless or overblown, microaggressions can have an extremely negative influence on the quality of life experienced by people from marginalized groups (Sue 2010).

Because microaggressions happen on a routine basis in a person's day-to-day experience, microaggressions add up over time. They result in confusion, anxiety, depression, and diminish self-confidence. Whether intentional or not, microaggressions send clear signals to our students about society's perceptions of them and their families. The message that microaggressions send to people is that their humanity is not fully accepted or respected. For example, take the opening story into consideration: Tamara knew her family did not fit the assignment, and she was confused about how to handle it. It was brave of Tamara to talk to her teacher, but not all students feel comfortable doing that. As teachers, we rarely design assignments or activities with the intention of exclusion, but pausing and reading the task for inclusion can help prevent students feeling like Tamara did.

Gender microaggressions occur so commonly in schools that we often aren't even aware of them. Some "subtle" examples include teachers dividing their class by gender, complimenting a girl only on her appearance rather than her accomplishments, teaching from texts written almost exclusively by and for cisgender heterosexual men, and excluding LGBTQ families by using heteronormative language to describe families. Furthermore, unconscious bias can include misgendering, deadnaming, and not using students' preferred pronouns. Certainly, asking invasive questions about body parts or whether someone has had gender affirmation surgeries is inappropriate, and without question, off limits in a school setting.

Implicit bias and microaggressions do not make us bad people. They demonstrate that we are all products of our society and culture. However, their existence does clearly indicate the importance of self-reflection so that we can all try to do better and create more equitable environments in our classrooms and schools for *all* students. To overcome our cultural conditioning and counteract our implicit biases, we must continually educate ourselves and be self-reflexive. No educator wants to hurt their students, and by understanding sex, gender, and sexuality more fully, we can protect students from unintentional hurt or offense. Our personal beliefs shouldn't limit our ability to respect and validate all our students' experiences. The first step to this goal is individual self-reflection and awareness.

Cultivating Self-Reflection and Awareness

Consider the example of Reggie, a kindergarten teacher who reads *The Story of Valentine's Day* to his class.

> Now that we know a little more about the history of this holiday, we're going to make our own Valentines to share with friends. You see in your workstations that

there are different colors of paper, markers, scissors, glue, and glitter. Decide who you want to make a valentine for and be creative.

As the other students get to work, Sophia approaches Reggie. "Mr. Williams, I have a problem. I know who I want to make my valentine's for, but I'm afraid I will get in trouble or other students will make fun of me."

"Why would they do that, Sophia?" Reggie asks. "You can make your valentine for anyone you want."

"I want to make my valentine for Talisha. I like Talisha, but in all the stories we read it only shows girls liking boys. Also, all of the stories we read only show white boys and white girls together. Since I'm a white girl and Talisha is a Black girl, is it bad for me to ask her to be my valentine?"

"Sophia, I understand what you are saying," responds Reggie. "Maybe the books we are reading in class are not showing how big love is. We can all like and love whomever we choose. Love is never bad. I think you should make your valentine for Talisha, and I will do a better job of finding books that show different types of love and different types of relationships in the future. In fact, I have a new book called *Love Makes a Family* that we can read together today after we finish making our valentines. Thank you, Sophia, for being brave enough to share your concerns with me, and I can't wait to see your valentine for Talisha!"

With Reggie's story in mind, let's pause and think about our own experiences with implicit bias and microaggressions.

- Have you ever experienced a microaggression? How did you feel at the time?
- How would it feel to experience microaggressions daily?
- What are some microaggressions you have heard or witnessed toward other people or groups? What implicit bias or beliefs are these microaggressions based on?

Depending on where you are in your own journey of personal awareness, there are several questions that you may also want to consider. Overall, the goal of self-reflection is to answer the question, "Who am I?" However, self-reflection is an ongoing and lifelong process. Luckily, there are some smaller questions that make up who we are, such as:

- What are my identities?
- What identities are most important to me and why?
- How do my identities intersect with one another?
- How do I see myself in relation to others, especially others with diverse identities?
- How do I know what I know; what shapes my reality and framework of understanding?

Remember, the way we begin to understand ourselves is usually in interaction with others. Through interaction we learn who we are and who we are not (Ortiz and Patton 2012) and why we interact with others in the ways that we do.

Counteracting Microaggression

If you experience a microaggression, the first rule of thumb is to take care of yourself. Seek support from your friends and allies. If you witness a microaggression, the first rule of thumb is to respond initially to the person who was harmed. Check in with them to find out if they're OK. Ask how you can support them, and what they would like to see happen.

Interrupting microaggression may call for direct confrontation, but it doesn't usually. Responses like "I'm not comfortable with what you said" or "Did you really just say that?" or "Where did you learn that?" or just "Ouch!" often bring enough conscious awareness to the behavior to interrupt it. Because microaggressions are so often unintentional, anyone can commit one. If you inadvertently commit a microaggression, it's normal to feel defensive at first, but a more appropriate response is to acknowledge the hurt you caused (because the harm is real whether you meant to cause harm or not), then apologize and try to do better in the future. When working with students, one activity you could try in the classroom is to have students examine scenarios of common microaggressions and generate potential solutions to respond appropriately to them.

The Importance of Names, Honorifics, and Pronouns

Unconscious bias reminds us that like a fish in the ocean, we may not be aware of the water we swim in. The gender binary and cis- and heteronormativity may be so ingrained in our consciousness that we take it for granted. One way these unconscious biases manifest is through the assumptions we make about names, honorifics, and pronouns. As we have discussed earlier, honoring students' chosen names and preferred pronouns makes a tremendous difference to them.

In a study of trans children, Travers (2018) argues, "Being called a 'boy' or a 'girl' and assigned correspondingly gendered names and pronouns are two of the dimensions of power that adults exercise over children and that shape how they experience their world." This quote demonstrates the stakes at play when it comes to names and pronouns. As adults, and as educators, we have the ability to exercise power over children and young people; however, feminist educators encourage pedagogical strategies that create democratic classrooms. A democratic classroom is a space where students and educators share power, and neither dominates the learning environment (hooks 1994). If you as an educator believe in teaching as a strategy to challenge inequality, or as bell hooks says, "as the practice of freedom," then honoring chosen names and pronouns are practical and important ways to begin your journey toward creating a more equitable classroom, and world.

Chosen Names

Names are important. This seems like an obvious statement, but many students continue to be misnamed, or deadnamed. Research shows that being misnamed can be extremely detrimental and distracting for students. Often within the trans community, the name a person was assigned at birth is referred to as their "dead name." Someone calling a trans person by the name they were assigned at birth after they have chosen a new name is called "deadnaming." This is a major problem within the trans community. Deadnaming is often used against trans people, both intentionally—as a form of discrimination and oppression—and unintentionally, by those who know a person is trans and chose not to use or forget to use their chosen name (Rogers 2020). Hence, deadnaming is a form of both overt discrimination and a microaggression—a subtle slight—used to demonstrate that a person is not fully accepted into society.

Learning students' chosen names (and how to pronounce them properly) is a critical way to show students you care about who they are. For trans and gender nonconforming students, allowing them to choose the name they go by in the classroom is especially significant. This shows that their teacher respects their gender identity and their ability to name themselves. A trans author, Brett Ray (2015), writes,

> I realize that knowing my own name has carried the most weight in my life story. Until I knew my own name, I was completely unable to name the big truths—good and bad—about myself; I was unable to be honest with myself. I couldn't name my passions, the parts of myself that I loved, or the parts of myself that I wished weren't real until I truly knew how to name myself.

Supporting students as they find and claim the names they choose can allow them to explore other identities in ways that may feel impossible under their given name, or dead name.

As the quote above explains, assigning children a gender, a name, and pronouns without giving them any agency to decide these important characteristics themselves is a way adults exercise power over children. While giving children names can be an important way of passing on family history, connecting children with their families, and is not something we are going to stop doing anytime soon, sometimes these names can cause harm if parents, families, and teachers are not willing to listen to children. When children are old enough to know that the name they were assigned does not fit with the view they have of themselves, adults must be willing to listen.

The ability to choose one's name is not only an issue for students, but it is also essential that teachers and administrators can choose their names and that those names are respected. Names on classroom doors, desks, nametags, etc., should reflect the chosen name of teachers and administrators.

Because our society still assumes that women will be the ones to change their last names following marriage, the issue of allowing teachers and administrators to choose the names they will go by is also essential for cisgender, heterosexual women. Some schools still force teachers to go by their legal names. Following divorce, this may mean that some women are forced to continue to carry the names of their ex-spouses or go through the costly and time-consuming legal process of changing their last name.

Honorifics

When it comes to honorifics—the words or titles we use to show respect or status in our society (such as Ms., Mrs., Mr., Miss, Dr., etc.)—it is important that these are also correct and align with the students', teachers', or administrators' gender identity. Since most honorifics in the English language are gendered, we must be sure to ask which honorifics a person prefers or create and use new gender-neutral ones. For teachers and administrators with PhDs, Dr. is an acceptable gender-neutral honorific. For other teachers and administrators, a gender-neutral option that has begun to be used recently is Mx. This honorific is often used by LGBTQ educators and indicates to students that they cannot assume someone's gender. It can also be used as a gender-neutral option if you do not know a person's chosen honorific; however, it is newer so may take some explanation. Explanation is a good thing because it can lead to conversation and education. When talking to students, we recommend using the students chosen name and not using honorifics. This eliminates an unnecessary gendering of students.

Even when we know a student's gender identity, honorifics can be problematic because they also imply the gender inequality between men and women. For boys and men, the only gendered honorific is Mr. On the contrary, for women the honorific varies based on age and marital status. Typically, for girls and even young women, we use Miss. For adult women who are unmarried or whose marital status we do not know, we usually use Ms. For adult married women, we use Mrs. These distinctions for women imply that there are different levels of status and respect based on age and marital status, but for men they always carry the same amount of status and respect regardless of age or marital status. Therefore, the use of honorifics is fundamentally about power and respect. One possible way to overcome these issues of inequality in honorifics would be by using Mx. for all adults, or not using honorifics at all since they are all about power. Schools could also allow everyone to go by their chosen first names or come up with some other variation to eliminate the gender inequality in current usage within the English language.

Pronouns

We use pronouns to refer to ourselves and others. Most of us were taught early that pronouns are binary and align with our gender. Boys and men use he/him/his, and girls and women use she/her/hers; but again, these "familiar pronouns reinforce a gender binary" (Pastel et al. 2019:43). What happens when someone doesn't identify as a boy or girl? What happens if we look at someone and are unsure of how they identify their gender? What problems can arise when we assume someone's pronouns?

In English, we do not have a commonly accepted third gender pronoun. Historically, he/him/his have been used as general pronouns in common usage to refer to and include all genders. This language is problematic in much the same way as terms like *man*kind, fire*man*, fresh*man* are. These terms are androcentric, or male-centered; they implicitly make everything patriarchal male seem universally human (Aulette, Wittner, and Barber 2015). This means that everything female, woman, or gender nonbinary becomes "other," or deviant. This is why you never hear someone refer to a group of students of various genders as, "Hey, gals!" in the same way they would say, "Hey, guys!"

Without a third gender pronoun option, gender nonbinary people must get creative. Today, in the United States, the most common pronouns for gender nonbinary people are they/them/theirs. If you are an English teacher, maybe you just thought to yourself, "NO! They/them/theirs is not a singular pronoun!" However, they/them/theirs has been used as a singular pronoun, and accepted by grammarians as such, for a long time. Without other options, gender nonbinary people have begun to use these pronouns since they are already known by English-speaking people. Another option, sometimes used in the United States, is a newer pronoun known as ze/zir/zirs. The chart below shows each of these pronouns used in examples. Additionally, as the chart explains, "these are not the only pronouns. There are infinite numbers of pronouns as new ones emerge in our language."

Gender Pronouns

Please note that these are not the only pronouns. There are an infinite number of pronouns as new ones emerge in our language. Always ask someone for their pronouns.

Subjective	Objective	Possessive	Reflexive	Example
She	Her	Hers	Herself	She is speaking. I listened to her. The backpack is hers.
He	Him	His	Himself	He is speaking. I listened to him. The backpack is his.
They	Them	Theirs	Themself	They are speaking. I listened to them. The backpack is theirs.
Ze	Hir/Zir	Hirs/Zirs	Hirself/Zirself	Ze is speaking. I listened to hir. The backpack is zirs.

FIGURE 2.2
Source: Free to use from the Trans Student Educational Resources

So, if everyone's pronouns are not obvious like we were taught, how do we learn peoples' gender pronouns? Here is a list of tips for learning pronouns that will help you get started (Stringer 2011):

- *Don't assume.* Sometimes you can guess pronouns based on how someone looks, but there is no way to be sure.
- *Ask.* "Nice to meet you. What pronoun do you go by?" OR "What pronoun does Dan use?" OR "How would you like me to address you?"
- *Use names or descriptions.* "Hillary went to the store and Hillary forgot milk." OR "The person in the red hat said..."
- *Use all-gender language.* Replace "ladies," or "young men," with "everyone," or "this person" or "Good morning, friends," "Nice to see you all," "How is everyone doing today?" "Welcome back, folks."
- *Invite people to share their pronouns if they feel comfortable doing so in programs and meetings.* "Let's introduce ourselves with our name, pronoun, and age." In virtual meetings, we can show students and colleagues how to add their pronouns to their names on their screens.

- *Think about safety.* If the place is crowded or might be unaccepting, ask in private or wait until later.
- *Mistakes happen.* If you make a mistake, correct yourself. Try not to draw a lot of attention to the mistake. (Remember this is a learning process and it is ok to make mistakes if your intention is in the right place.)
- *Therefore, ask for patience, and be patient.* Let people know you're trying, and understand if someone reacts to your mistake.
- *Make it a personal priority.* Correct pronouns increase safety and acceptance. Be diligent and attentive.
- *Practice, practice, practice!* The more you think about pronouns, the easier it is to learn them.

Overall, as educators, our job is to model what we hope to see from our students. And when students are struggling with a concept or experience, it also can lead to a teachable moment. Be an example by attempting to make your language more inclusive and normalizing talk about pronouns. There are several ways to do this. For one, with every opportunity we as teachers are asked to use our names, we can also offer our pronouns. This can include but is not limited to name tags, desk tags, email signature lines, and even when using a virtual format, on the screen.

We can also ask students what pronouns they prefer to use, paying attention to how, when, and for whom it is safe to ask. By asking the pronouns of all students, we can normalize this process, and this makes society more equitable. If you are using name tags or desk name tents, it is also very helpful to include pronouns on these items. This helps us practice and remember to use people's chosen names and pronouns. In fact, making name tents for their desks with their gender pronouns on them is a great way to start a new class. Even if all of the students choose the pronouns you would have guessed, they now know that this matters to you and that gender is something we cannot assume. In doing our best to respect students' choices, we create a safer and more comfortable environment for our students.

When Martha and Dr. Dietra Hawkins were co-facilitating a virtual professional development workshop on trauma-informed pedagogy with a group of mental health professionals, a school psychologist asked Dietra why she had added the pronouns, she/her, to her screen name. When Martha and Dr. Dietra Hawkins were co-facilitating a virtual professional development workshop on trauma-informed pedagogy with a group of mental health professionals, a school psychologist asked Dietra why she had added the pronouns, she/her, to her screen name. She answered:

> I add them as a sign of solidarity. Even though my pronouns signify that I am a cigender woman, they also signify that I am aware that other gender identities exist and are likely here in the room with me. It shows that I accept, honor, and affirm their identities.

Martha added that honoring students' chosen names and preferred pronouns has profound implications for their mental health. As the Trevor Project (2021) reveals, trans and nonbinary youth who have their chosen pronouns respected by important people in their lives attempted suicide at half the rates of youth who reported that their preferred pronouns were not respected. Another participant thanked the facilitators for this information. She explained, "I am working with a trans student right now, and this makes it clear how important it is for me to use the right pronouns when I refer to them. I will definitely make this a priority!" Simply by adding their own pronouns, Dietra and Martha created a "teachable moment" for school professionals who until then were unfamiliar with the importance of gender pronouns. Using a student's chosen name and preferred pronouns when referring to them empowers them with a sense of agency over their own experience.

Dean Spade, a trans activist, writer, and law school professor at UCLA, provides a sample introduction to an activity called "pronoun go-rounds" that makes the topic of pronoun usage educational and meaningful. Feel free to edit the introduction to fit your needs—such as the age and understanding level of your students. Here is the sample introduction (Spade 2018):

> At gatherings of many kinds, people do go-rounds to share their names with one another. Knowing what people like to be called is a key part of talking and relating with them. When we talk in groups, we not only refer to people by names, but also by pronouns. For example, a participant might say "I'd like to hear from Fatima. I think she has the information we are looking for." Or "I agree with Sam and I think we should talk in more detail about his proposal."
>
> We want to make sure that people refer to each other by the name and pronoun that the person goes by. Frequently people assume they know what pronoun a person goes by based on looking at them. When we guess at people's pronouns we might get them wrong. When people's pronouns are mistaken they may feel uncomfortable and be less likely to participate in the group. We want everyone to participate here, and we want everyone to know how to refer to each other respectfully. So when we go around, each person is invited to share their name and information about what pronoun they go by. Some people may use "he/him/his," "she/her/hers," some may prefer to be referred to just by their names and not have a pronoun used, some people use "they/them/theirs" as a gender neutral-pronoun, and some people use gender-neutral pronouns that may be new to some people in this room, such as "ze/hir/hirs" or others, and some people are open to being called by more than one set of pronouns. Please listen closely to each other and remember that if you forget what someone said later, you can ask them to remind you before you refer to them. It's better to ask than to refer to someone by something they don't like to go by. This exercise is important to help everyone in this room participate and avoid unintentionally disrespecting each other, so please take it seriously and listen carefully.

We add a note of caution here and emphasize that while we encourage you to explore the topic of pronouns with your students, you should be careful that you are *inviting* and not compelling them to share their pronouns. By explaining the gendered usage of pronouns and why we don't want to assume pronouns, we can begin a discussion that makes it safe for some students to disclose how they identify. Consider, however, that some students may be in the process of grappling with their gender identities and may not be ready or willing to disclose how they identify themselves or they may simply not know.

For instance, Margot, a white, cisgender, heterosexual teacher in a progressive independent school, considered herself a gender ally. She introduced the topics of gendered pronouns to her students and asked them to create name plates specifying the pronouns they prefer. When one of her students, Chris, didn't complete their name plate and didn't come to school the next day, Margot called Chris's parents. She learned that Chris was involved in a very personal struggle with their identity at the time and did not feel safe or ready to share this information with his teacher or classmates. It was two years later that Chris revealed to his teachers and classmates that they identified as nonbinary and preferred they/them/theirs pronouns.

Learning and Practicing Pronouns: An Activity

Here is an activity adapted from the Gay-Straight Alliance for Safe Schools (GSAFE). You can find numerous other resources for educators working with issues of gender and sexuality on their site: https://gsafewi.org. For this activity, you will need at least two people and some reading material. This activity can be done either in pairs or in a larger group.

Start by asking students to grab a book they are reading either for a class or for fun. Choose reading material based on age and reading level. Novels with a lot of character descriptions and narrative would work best, as they will have the most subject, object, and possessive pronouns. Scan the pages to find a section with a lot of pronouns and ask for a volunteer to go first.

One at a time, have students read aloud for 30 seconds, replacing all the gendered pronouns (she/her/hers and he/him/him) with gender-neutral or gender-inclusive pronouns (they/them/theirs or ze/zir/zirs). If the reader accidentally misses a pronoun, the group will have the opportunity to *politely* correct them. Part of being a good ally to trans people is letting others know when they use an incorrect pronoun or when they say something that might be offensive to the trans community. The responsibility of encouraging gender-neutral and trans-inclusive language should not rest solely with trans individuals.

Remember: Not everyone is comfortable reading aloud, and students should be able to opt out of this activity. Students who don't want to read out loud could be the timekeepers or scan other books for the next section to read.

Mistakes Will happen

Maybe now you are thinking, "But what if I get it wrong?" This is likely to happen and it is ok! It happened to Margot and it happens to us all the time. There are few things you need to remember about "messing up." First, if you mess up and realize it, this means you are trying, which is more than a lot of people are doing. Most people who go by preferred pronouns genuinely appreciate the effort, even if you forget and make a mistake sometimes.

Here are a few tips for when we mess up:

- If the mistake just happened, it's okay to say, "I'm sorry, I meant to say…" The key here is not drawing a lot of attention to the mistake or making the person whose pronoun you messed up to feel more uncomfortable.
- If you realize you messed up a little later, it is appropriate to apologize and let them know you are trying to do better. Again, don't make it a big deal, but show you care.
- If you are unsure if you've made a mistake, it is always good to ask. One way to do this is to say something like,

"I'm trying to do better with gender pronouns. My pronouns are he/him/his. May I ask for your pronouns?"
- Finally, if you hear someone else make a mistake, there are several ways to respond. Most importantly, make sure you are not putting the person whose pronouns were misstated in a bad or unsafe position. Sometimes, depending on the situation, it is best to let it go and let the person correct the party in error themselves. In an educational setting, hopefully, you feel comfortable educating your colleagues on students' and faculties' pronouns. You could respond using the correct pronouns, without bringing extra attention to the issue. Alternatively, you could use an educational approach with a colleague, even providing them with resources, like the chart above, if they are willing to listen.
- For more resources and examples on all the topics discussed regarding pronouns, check out Mypronouns.org

Conclusion

The way we see our students impacts how they see themselves, how they relate to school, and how well they learn. Our affinity bias may cause us to be more accepting of students we share common experiences with, and our confirmation bias may allow them to connect with us more easily when they see themselves in us (Frame 2021). Teachers need to be humble and recognize that their perspectives may be influenced by their social location. Listening to the voices of our students is a crucial aspect of this work, and most especially, listening to the voices of our most vulnerable students—students whose gender and sexual identities fall outside of the expectations of our society. School is full of opportunities for both inclusion and disenfranchisement, and as teachers, we are called upon to design opportunities for inclusion. This process begins with an awareness of unconscious bias and how it manifests on personal, interactional, and institutional levels.

3

Interactional Experiences of Gender and Sexuality in the Classroom and Schools

FIGURE 3.1
Source: JackF

How do gender and sexuality influence your interactions with students in the classroom? What are you teaching students about gender and sexuality, even in classes that seem to have nothing to do with these topics? How do your interactions

DOI: 10.4324/9781003125310-4

with students' parents, guardians, and families relate to gender and sexuality? Should lesbian, gay, bisexual, trans, and other queer (LGBTQ) teachers and administrators be "out" and open to students? In this chapter, we will discuss these issues and explore how gender and sexuality are always relevant, central topics despite grade level or course. We examine teachers' interactions with students in the classroom and beyond, as well as with students' families and the broader education system. We provide information on classroom management and curriculum while demonstrating the importance of taking an intersectional approach to all student interactions.

Gender and sexuality intersect with both the formal and hidden curriculum in your classroom, and student outcomes vary greatly depending on other characteristics, such as race, class, and ability. It is important for teachers to be conscious of the interactions of gender and sexuality and strive to have an inclusive curriculum. To begin, as educators, we should consider our own identities, and how these interact and influence student learning. For teachers who are openly LGBTQ and must decide whether to come out in their classrooms, the stakes may be even higher. As discussed in the previous chapter, the importance of inclusive language, including gender-neutral terminology and the use of chosen names, honorifics, and pronouns, are vital issues in affirming students' identities. Finally, the significance of teachers' interactions with students' parents, guardians, and families cannot be overemphasized. Families are the primary institution of socialization; where children first come to learn about the social world around them. This heavily influences classroom dynamics and relationships. Let's begin by thinking about how to manage an intersectional and inclusive classroom and school. We hope that this is a goal for all educators, as an inclusive classroom is vital to all students' learning regardless of gender and sexuality.

Managing an Intersectional and Inclusive Classroom and School

Curriculum Concerns

Teachers are trained extensively on how to teach the formal curriculum. Formal curriculum is the subject matter you are trying to convey to students (e.g., math, social studies, sociology, biology), and it has clearly stated goals and objectives (Thompson and Armato 2012). Unfortunately, most teacher education programs to date have not spent adequate time training teachers on the hidden curriculum or the "hidden agenda" of the education system (Illich 1983; Thompson and Armato 2012). As Thompson and Armato (2012:113 *emphasis in original*) explain, "In addition to formal curriculum… young people also encounter a *hidden curriculum*, unstated values, beliefs, and assumptions embedded in the subject matter, and *pedagogical strategies*, the ways through which people are taught and are expected to learn." Hence, the unstated values, beliefs, and assumptions of the curriculum are transferred to students through teaching styles and pedagogical strategies. Hidden values can take the form of unconscious bias as in when teachers call on boys more frequently than girls to answer questions in class or when teachers communicate their unspoken expectation that boys will perform better than girls in math and science.

Historically, teachers were trained to use a banking model of teaching in which they provide subject area content information to students, using textbooks and lectures (Freire 1970). Students were asked to acquire subject matter information and then recite it back to the teacher. Within this pedagogical strategy, as well as within the hidden values, beliefs, and assumptions of different subjects, many "unwritten lessons" are conveyed to students based on what behaviors are rewarded and punished (Aulette and Wittner 2015:169; Illich 1983). While a wide array of research has shown this pedagogical strategy is not the best for genuine learning, standardized testing and formal assessment or evaluation continue to force some teachers to teach students in this way. In this book, we urge those teaching the next generation to strive for a more generative curriculum and use pedagogical strategies that take seriously how the hidden curriculum of education impacts students' lives beyond the tests.

This hidden curriculum is particularly relevant in terms of gender and sexuality. While the formal curriculum of K-12 education rarely directly teaches students about gender and sexuality, the hidden curriculum clearly communicates to students the assumption that to be "normal" in society you must be cisgender (cisnormativity) and heterosexual (heteronormativity). These norms are communicated in the stories they read, the posters on the walls, and in the role models they see surrounding them. The hidden curriculum also conveys a gender binary structure in which (cis) women and (cis) men are fundamentally different based on their sex and gender. This hidden curriculum is "conveyed in patterns of who is present or absent and the framework of presentation" (Thompson and Armato 2012:113), as well as in the language we use in the classroom more broadly.

For instance, if all the examples of families in your class' textbooks, children's literature, and classroom examples are of heterosexual couples with children, this communicates to students that most families look this way and families who do not (if they exist) are "other." Similarly, if all the examples of women used in your class relate to household and family responsibilities, while the examples of men relate to work outside of the home and family, these messages teach students that men and women are essentially different and have different roles in society.

Spence, a sixth-grade science teacher, was concerned about the achievement gap between boys and girls in science, technology, engineering, and math (STEM) that he saw playing out in his classroom. Low-performing students, often girls and students of color, told him that science was boring and checked out during his lessons. When he looked around his classroom, he realized that his textbooks, library books, and the posters on his walls overwhelmingly displayed images of white men portrayed as scientists. "Most people think of science as the domain of white men," Spence said, "But I knew my students needed to 'see themselves' in the curriculum. It wasn't hard to find ways to represent more diversity because all kinds of people do science." Spence hung posters of scientists of color, women, and LGBTQ scientists on the walls, he updated his class library with books reflecting scientists with diverse identities, and he challenged students to research scientists with a diversity of identities. He used his classroom walls to launch inquiries into the role of race and gender identities in science learning, exploring the implications of identity in the achievement gap in STEM subjects and raising questions about explicit, implicit, and internalized biases in science. His students created avatars of themselves to display on an "inclusion wall" with rainbow colors, so they were surrounded by images that looked like them and reflected their personal and social identities. In addition to representing his students' identities in his classroom, Spence's strategies for inclusion transformed his relationships with his students because they recognized him as a trusted advocate.

In addition to who is and is not present in our class materials and the language we use in the classroom, many times students are divided in the classroom based on gender, even when it is an irrelevant characteristic (which is almost always). As Aulette and Wittner (2015:142) discuss, "Differential treatment begins with a segregation of children by gender that is done automatically and with little thought." While most teachers divide students along the lines of gender unconsciously and with no malice, this division leads schools to continue "to create the dichotomy of boys and girls" (Aulette and Wittner 2015:142). Usually, when a group is divided into two different categories, those categories are treated differently and unequally. Also, this often leads to competition and animosity between the groups. Research has clearly shown that this is the case with gender in education.

The separation of students based on gender—boys on one side and girls on the other—leads teachers to respond very differently to each group. For example, teachers respond to boys more; wait less time for girls to reply before interrupting them with the answer; pay more attention to boys; allow boys to speak out of turn; engage in fewer complex interactions with girls; are more likely to comment on girls' appearance or clothing; and praise boys more (Aulette and Wittner 2015). Furthermore, this method of dividing the class leaves trans and gender-nonconforming students to choose between the two groups, which can be damaging and even dangerous to their identity development and sense of self.

The good and bad news here is that teachers are usually not conscious of the bias and discrimination inherent in traditional curriculum and pedagogical strategies (Aulette and Wittner 2015). In fact, some studies have shown that teachers are often shocked to see how they treat students differently based on gender when they view themselves teaching on video (Aulette and Wittner 2015; Ridgway and Healy 1997; Sadker and Sadker 1994). This means, by becoming more conscious of these biases, teachers can overcome many of these issues and change the classroom environment to be more inclusive and fairer. This is paramount because when teachers allow unconscious biases to dominate the classroom and are not conscious of the marginalization that can occur because of the textbooks and reading materials they choose, "they may create and reinforce a *chilly climate*, an environment whereby gender and other dimensions of social inequality create differentially welcoming classroom experiences for different groups of people" (Thompson and Armato 2012:114).

For instance, trans students may feel that they are alone and no one else is like them. Mori, a transfeminine student said, "When I go into a classroom for the first time, I like to see rainbow colors. I know then that the teacher has thought about people like me." Or students being raised by single parents may feel like their family is lacking in some way because all of the families presented in class look different from their own. Girls may begin to believe they should not pursue a career in math because boys are always shown in the textbook, and the teacher reinforces this idea by behaving in ways that make it seem that boys are naturally better at math.

FIGURE 3.2
Source: Imgorthand

To take this last example a step further, when teachers associate math with masculinity, they allow boys to rate themselves as more competent in math, and this often leads them to pursue further education and career paths in math-related fields (Aulette and Witter 2015). This is obviously problematic because it may hold back equally competent or even more competent girls from pursuing careers in math or related disciplines. This is also detrimental because career fields that are coded as masculine, such as STEM, usually produce higher salaries than those coded as feminine. The gender bias in K-12 education can end up following students their entire life and impacting their earning potential. If men are thought to be better at the jobs that pay more, gender income inequality continues long after completing one's education.

The hidden curriculum, biased pedagogical strategies, and the chilly climate also relate to creating self-fulfilling prophecies through education. Self-fulfilling prophecies are situations where teachers believe that a student or group of students will outperform another student or group of students based on unrelated characteristics or traits, such as gender, sexuality, race, ethnicity, ability, etc. (Thompson and Armato 2012). For example, if teachers believe that boys will do better in math, then they give boys more attention and resources in math courses. This results in boys doing better than girls in math and fulfilling the prediction that boys are better than girls at math. However, this gap in math ability disappears when girls and boys are treated equally in the classroom and given equal resources. By simply acknowledging our gender biases and working to overcome them, we can begin to make schools more inclusive immediately and begin to eradicate gender inequality in our society more broadly.

The well-documented concept of *stereotype threat* and its impact on the performance of women and girls in STEM subjects is related to the self-fulfilling prophecy (Good, Aronson, and Harder 2008; Good, Rattan, and Dweck 2012; Picho, Rodriguez, and Finnie 2013). Stereotype threat occurs when students confront situations in which they are at risk of confirming a negative stereotype about their social group. Research has shown that when women and girls are primed with the idea that gender identity impacts test scores, they score significantly lower than men and boys. However, when told that gender doesn't affect performance on a particular test, they score slightly higher than men and boys. All students benefit from learning to identify and deconstruct gender stereotypes. This empowerment has an equalizing effect on status for all students (Steele and Cohn-Vargas 2013).

Steele and Cohn-Vargas (2013) emphasize the importance of teachers monitoring classroom dynamics, as the social/political dynamics in society are often mirrored in the classroom. Teachers who openly challenge gender role stereotypes interrupt these negative dynamics. We can affirm all of our students' intelligence, competency, and capacity for learning. We can introduce materials and provide role models that counteract stereotypes and reduce stereotype threats. Finally, we can teach students to counteract stereotype threats within themselves. Simply knowing that the concept exists helps them begin to protect themselves from its impact. They can learn to formulate questions and reevaluate notions they may have internalized about their gendered identities. This helps them learn not only to critique their own behavior but also what they see in the world around them. Elliot (2015:140) writes, "By claiming your intelligence, you are manifesting what will happen to you."

Race in the Classroom

Noticeably, gender and sexuality are not the only identities that influence the students in your classroom. Each student has a variety of identities that intersect to create unique situations and life chances. For an illustration of how gender and race intersect in the classroom, generally, white boys get the most attention in school from teachers, followed by boys of color, then white girls, with girls of color receiving the least amount of teacher attention (Aulette and Wittner 2015). To amplify this point, research conducted by Monique Morris (2016) demonstrates how much more harshly Black girls are treated in school and the harmful effects that come from such experiences. Therefore, simply saying that boys get more attention in the classroom ignores the importance of race in this interaction.

Here, we use mathematics and reading proficiencies to provide an example of how race intersects with gender when it comes to educational outcomes. As discussed, teachers show the greatest bias against girls in math and science courses (Aulette and Wittner 2015). Due to this bias, boys have historically outperformed girls in mathematics proficiency in K-12 education (Child Trends 2019; Thompson and Armato 2012). Overall, in the United States, math scores increased on average from 1990 until they peaked in 2013. Because both boys and girls scores increased at similar rates until 2013, the gap between boys and girls scores remains. By 2017, boys continued to outscore girls in math, but only slightly (Child Trends 2019). For instance, in eighth grade, boys scored on average 283 versus girls scoring 282 (Child Trends 2019). However, when race and ethnicity were factored in, the gaps in mathematics proficiency were much more complex and pronounced. While scores for all racial groups improved from 1990 to 2017, the gaps based on race and ethnicity also remained (Child Trends 2019). Here is what those numbers looked like in 2017 for eighth graders based on race: scoring the highest at 310 were Asian/Pacific Islander students, followed by white students at 293, then Hispanic students at 269, American Indian students at 267, and with the lowest scores, Black students with an average of 260 (Child Trends 2019).

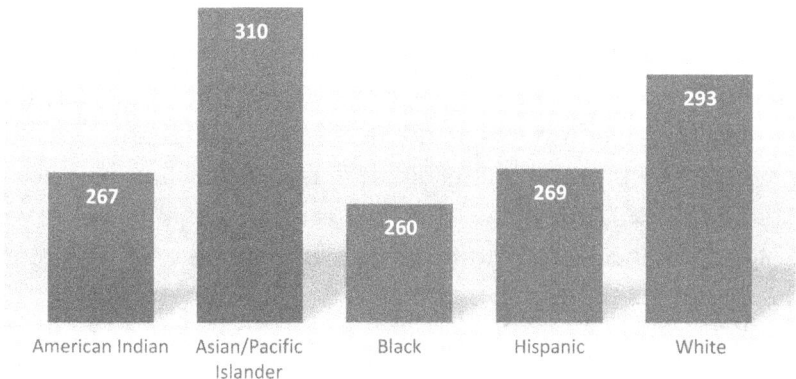

FIGURE 3.3 2017 Eighth Grade Math Scores by Race
Source: From research presented in Brey, Cristobal de Brey, Lauren Musu, Joel McFarland, Sidney Wilkinson-Flicker, Melissa Diliberti, Anlan Zhang, Claire Branstetter, and Xiaolei Wang. 2019. Status and Trends in the Education of Racial and Ethnic Groups 2018. National Center for Education Statistics. https://nces.ed.gov/pubs2019/2019038.pdf

We can clearly see the results of the chilly climate and self-fulfilling prophecies here, along with other institutional barriers—which we will discuss more fully in Chapter 5. In terms of gender, the belief that boys are better at math keeps them outperforming girls. In terms of race, stereotypes about Asian Americans being better at math often lead teachers to give them more attention and resources, while beliefs that

Black students will be weaker in math lead them to give Black students fewer resources and less attention (Chou 2012; Chou and Feagin 2014; Chou, Lee and Ho 2015).

The gender trend is reversed when it comes to reading proficiency—a skill attributed to girls rather than boys. In the eighth grade, girls outperform boys in reading scores with an average score of 272 to boys' score of 262 (Child Trends 2019). In 2017, reading proficiency by race showed similar patterns to mathematics proficiency. Asian/Pacific Islander students had the highest reading scores, followed by white students, then Hispanic students, American Indian students, and again Black students held the lowest level of proficiency (Child Trends 2019). Unconscious race bias on the part of teachers has major influences on students' scores in both math and reading (Chou 2012; Chou, Lee, and Ho 2015). In addition to the lack of culturally responsive teaching strategies, the assumption that American Indian and Black students are the least competent in school results in this self-fulfilling prophecy. Again, this is also highly related to rates of poverty and other historic instances of institutional racism that we will explore in the institutional chapter.

A 2016 study from Yale Child Study Center (https://medicine.yale.edu/childstudy/zigler/publications/Preschool%20Implicit%20Bias%20Policy%20Brief_final_9_26_276766_5379_v1.pdf) used eye-tracking technology to measure which students' preschool teachers watched most closely when challenging behaviors were anticipated. The study showed that teachers tracked Black boys 42 percent of the time, white boys 34 percent, Black girls 10 percent, and white girls 13 percent. Teachers' expectations of misbehavior and consequent observations of students based on gender and race identities may help explain why we continue to see gender and race disparities in school discipline outcomes.

Poverty in the Classroom

Nearly one in seven children in the United States is poor (The State of America's Children 2021), and the socioeconomic status of children's families is the clearest indicator of how well they will perform in school. Ball (2010) suggests that between 9 and 15 percent of academic performance can be explained by what happens in school, and class background explains the rest. A Georgetown University study found that disparities between achievement and socioeconomic status are apparent by the time a child enters kindergarten, and these disparities track students well into adulthood (Carnevale, Fasules, Quinn, and Campbell 2019). There are exceptions, of course, but studies overwhelmingly show that students from affluent backgrounds perform better in school than students from low-income homes (Carnevale et al. 2019; Cunha and Heckman 2009; Heckman 2008; Lanahan 2009; McLanahan and Percheski 2008; Putnam 2015).

The policies dictating public school funding play a role in perpetuating inequities. Public school funding is not distributed equally as it reflects property values that are rooted in historical segregation practices (Carter 2005; Kendi 2016; Schwalbe 2014). Consequently, students' educational experiences are shaped by where they live and their family's access to resources.

For some students, school is the most consistent source of security. The data on free and reduced lunch (Digest of Education Statistics 2012) reveal complicated patterns of inequality. These patterns demonstrate at what rates and in which locations reduced or free lunch is needed, showing that many students rely on school for more than education, but also basic needs. This data also demonstrate that society embodies social inequality in schooling by reflecting which populations have access to opportunities as well as access to needs.

Ability in the Classroom

FIGURE 3.4
Source: Marco VDM

Recently, studies have begun to show a shift in how teachers treat boys in school, and much of this is related to the diagnosis—and overdiagnosis—of learning disabilities or differences. The intersections with gender and ability in the classroom have led some teachers to devalue boys in the classroom (Aulette and Wittner 2015). While girls are catching up with boys in mathematics proficiency—albeit slowly, boys still trail behind girls in reading proficiency. Some of this difference can be attributed to higher rates of diagnosis of attention deficit and hyperactivity disorder (ADHD) and the unconscious biases that teachers hold about boys being more hyperactive and more likely to get into trouble.

Regarding the intersections of ability and gender, the diagnosis—or what some argue is an overdiagnosis—of ADHD, especially for boys, is a major issue in education today. In the 1990s, diagnosis of ADHD increased by 700 percent (Rafalovich 2005), and this rate nearly doubled again by 2016—from 6.1 percent in 1997–1998 to 10.2 percent in 2015–2016 (Xu, Strathearn, Liu, Yang, and Bao 2018). While rates of ADHD diagnosis have increased for girls, the rate of boys diagnosed remains more than double that of the rate of girls diagnosed (Xu et al. 2018). Historically, ADHD was seen as a white, middle-class, boys' disorder, but in 2016, the percentage of Black students diagnosed was slightly higher than the number of white students diagnosed (12.8 percent compared to 12.0 percent, respectively) (Xu et al. 2018).

While there is still a lot to learn about ADHD, some scholars "worry that ADHD is an excuse for medicating children, especially boys, for behavior that is in the normal range or is caused by social factors rather than neurological ones" (Aulette and Witter 2015:147). Specifically, Hart, Grant, and Riley (2006) suggest that our culture sends double and mixed messages to boys. We expect boys to be active, assertive, outspoken, and strong, yet in school, we ask them to sit quietly for long periods of time and then wonder why they "misbehave." This is overly problematic at schools where physical education and playtime outside have been cut or restricted. Overall, these examples demonstrate why an inclusive curriculum is critical to ensuring gender equality in education.

A Move to Inclusive Curriculum

FIGURE 3.5
Source: FatCamera

Now that we have laid out some of the biased practices that can happen in the classroom, we want to provide some ideas about how to move away from these problematic and oftentimes exclusive practices and offer suggestions that will welcome students. When considering the curriculum for any course, teachers must be mindful of how and in what ways a diversity of material is presented. Whether the course is directly dealing with gender or sexuality, noninclusive language is always an issue. For example, if you are teaching a math class and all your examples involve a little boy named John Smith, the language tells the class something about your beliefs, even if unconscious, about math or at least, implies that boys are what comes to mind when thinking about math. Therefore, teachers must be conscious of the language, examples, and images they use in all courses.

The issue of language is especially important when considering gender and sexuality because often teachers are not fully trained or aware of the appropriate, affirming, and up-to-date language. In fact, if teachers are not

> made aware of and given permission to confidently use *appropriate* language describing LGBT+ identities.... Young people who are very intuitive will pick up on it, leading some who may already be aware of their own LGBT+ identity (or those with LGBT+ friends and family) to begin suspecting that there is something shameful about their selves.
>
> (Dellenty 2019:94)

This can be difficult with the continuous shifting of language, but what is necessary is that all teachers and administrators work to stay up-to-date on language and are open to making mistakes and learning new language. Humility is key; it is ok to make mistakes and to let your students know that you are also still learning. We must let our students know, while we may be experts in the subject—the formal curriculum—we are teaching, this does not mean that we are experts in everything. Teachers are human beings. Teachers make mistakes, and there is always room for growth and change.

For example, a term that was once accepted, but is now perceived as problematic by most LGBTQ people is "lifestyle." The term lifestyle is often used in religious contexts to devalue LGBTQ peoples' identities and to imply that they *choose* their identities freely (Dellenty 2019). The term holds negative connotations for many LGBTQ people, and therefore, by simply avoiding this term, you can ensure that you do not offend someone. Additionally, as Dellenty (2019:29) explains, "Even if our young people were 'choosing' to identity as LGBT+, our duty of care would still stand."

It can be very difficult to remove gendered and cis- and heteronormative language from our vocabulary because we were all socialized in a sexist, cisnormative, heteronormative society. As Pastel et al. (2019:142) explain, "Whether or not we think we're talking about gender, we're talking about gender because binary gender runs throughout our language." Despite the difficulties, and often discomforts, that come with changing our language to be more inclusive, this is one of the most important individual and interactional level changes we can each make to ensure that our students feel accepted and welcomed.

Pastel et al. (2019) provide an excellent chart of gendered language and some inclusive alternatives. In their book, *Supporting Gender Diversity in Early Childhood Classrooms* (2019), it is recommended to adapt the list to fit your own needs, specifically with words and phrases you commonly use that are gendered, and some alternatives to practice. On pages 80–81, we provide our version of this table, with additional examples of heteronormative and transphobic language and some inclusive alternatives. Remember, language is always changing, so be sure to update this table and make sure that it is relevant to the local vocabulary and speech patterns of your region.

TABLE 3.1 Common Gendered and Heteronormative Language and Some Inclusive Alternatives

Instead of...	Try...
"Boys and girls," "ladies and gentlemen," "you guys"	Children, students, kids, everyone, everybody, folks, you all
"Look at the girl over there. She has cool shoes."	"Look at that student over there. They have cool shoes." (Don't assign gender to strangers.)
"He's a hungry little caterpillar."	"It's a hungry little caterpillar!" (Or "she," or "they"; resist defaulting to male gender on every animal and inanimate object.)
"Boys have penises, girls have vaginas."	"Many boys have penises, some don't. Many girls have vaginas, some don't." (Body parts do not equal gender.)
"You were born a girl." "He was born a girl."	"When you were born, adults guessed you were a girl. You get to decide if that is true." "When he was born, people assumed he was a girl, but they were incorrect. He is a boy."
"She is such a pretty girl." "He is so strong."	"He is pretty and intelligent." "She is strong and smart." (Purposely switch gendered compliments.)
"Is that a boy or a girl?" "Are you a boy or girl?"	"I don't know. If they were a friend of ours, we could ask them." "No, I'm just me."
"The student is a transsexual." "My student is a trans." "The transgenders need a separate bathroom."	"I have a student who identifies as transgender." "My student is trans." "Transgender people need a place to safely use the restroom in this building." (Never use "a [fill in the blank]" or pluralize an identity. Some people use transsexual but be sure before you assign this identity to someone based on assumption.)
"I have two homosexual students." "I do not understand people who live a homosexual lifestyle."	"In my class, I have students of various sexualities, one student identifies as gay and another as bisexual." "I need to do more work to become educated about sexuality. I am unclear about the various terminology."
"My male student keeps putting on dresses at play time; he must be a transvestite."	"I have a student who was presumed to be a boy when he was born but likes to wear dresses at play time." (Putting on dresses doesn't mean anything and the more appropriate identity today for people who are cisgender but like to wear clothes typical to another gender is cross dresser, not transvestite.)

"I have a student whose parents are in a gay relationship."	"I have a student whose parents are in a same-sex relationship. I should ask him what he calls each of his parents so I make sure to get it correct at the parent-teacher conference." (You could ask all of your students about their families and what they call those they care about. Normalize that families vary.)
"I wonder if that trans had a sex change."	"That person said they identify as transgender, but it is none of my business if they have or plan to have gender affirmation surgeries." (There is no such thing as a trans. Rather than using trans as a noun, use it as an adjective to describe a person, people, or individual(s) with the identity. No one identity encompasses a person.)
"My student is a he-she."	"My student was assumed to be a boy when they were born, but now presents as gender nonconforming."
"OK class, tell me about your mother and father."	"OK class, tell me about who you live with." "OK class, tell me about your parents or guardians." (Don't assume all families are heterosexual or have two parents.)

Voices in the Curriculum and Classroom

FIGURE 3.6
Source: Massonstock

As stated earlier and reemphasized here, it is important that diverse voices and perspectives are heard and seen in the images and examples used in our classrooms. This is particularly important for historically excluded gender and sexual minorities who are often rendered invisible in the curriculum and the education system. There are many ways to make LGBTQ voices heard and seen across K-12 education. Teachers can ensure that the materials they choose for their classes are not all written by white, heterosexual, cisgender men. Teachers can scan textbooks for diverse images: girls doing science, families with single dads, or a same-sex couple holding hands. Do you use PowerPoints or some type of presentation in your class? If so, are the images you choose diverse and inclusive of a variety of types of people and families? Also, be sure to think about the posters that hang in your classroom or school. Do they send a message to your students about what is normal? Teachers can also bring gender and sexual diversity into their classrooms through guest speakers or take students on field trips that expand their ideas.

All of these examples create more inclusive classrooms, and as a bonus, they will make the curriculum more interesting. Teachers frequently incorporate material from posters on their walls, and the effect can allow students to see and think of topics from more than just one perspective. Even if the subject seemingly has nothing to do with gender and sexuality, it is still possible to ensure that the classroom is inclusive. Make sure that the examples you use for math problems include girls and nonbinary people. Put pictures of women chemists and transgender biologists in your presentations. Choose textbooks for anatomy that include discussion of intersexuality. And make sure that sex education includes everyone, not just Christian, heterosexual, and cisgender students.

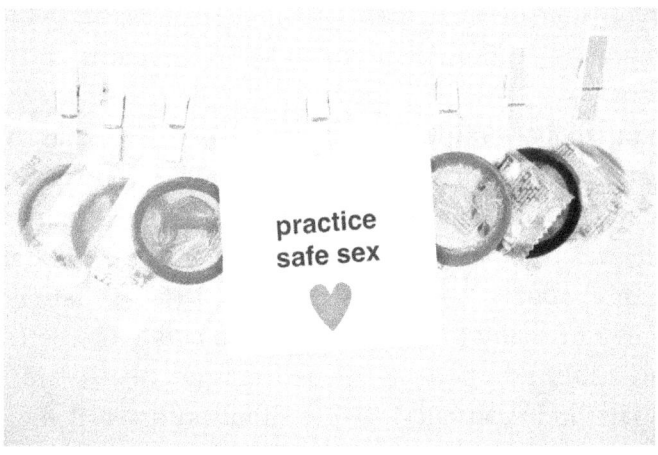

FIGURE 3.7
Source: CatLane

When thinking about interactional experiences of gender and sexuality in the classroom, teachers must also remain aware of the diversity of families in our society today. It is inappropriate to assume what type of family your students have and, therefore, it is vital to ensure that diverse families are part of your curriculum. In Shaun Dellenty's (2019:34) book, *Celebrating Difference: A Whole School Approach to LGBT+ Inclusion*, they explain:

> In our 21st-century world, families come in a variety of shapes and sizes. In discussing family groups with school stakeholders, we must no longer assume that a marriage is between a woman and a man, or that LGBT+ people cannot have children, or that a parent in a male-female partnership cannot be transgender, or indeed that a transgender man cannot have periods or a baby.

Dellenty goes on to suggest that all teachers and administrators work under the assumption that there are LGBTQ people present in our classrooms and schools, or at the very least there are students who have LGBTQ friends and family members.

Under this assumption, it is even more vital that our language and curriculum are always as inclusive as possible. Family is fundamental to children. As Dellenty (2019:130) argues, all children "need to be able to speak about and feel pride in their own family group or network of affection." Since all families look different, and many (or most) have members who are LGBTQ, Dellenty (2019:130) goes as far as to argue, "If we are unable to validate and celebrate [diverse families] (even if the nature of their parental structure is at odds with our personal beliefs) then we are simply in the wrong job."

Teachers–Out in the Classroom?

Coming out (sometimes referred to as coming out of the closet) is the process of revealing one's sexual and/or gender identity to self and others. Coming out is a process that is never complete. Dellenty (2019:99) explains:

> LGBT+ people don't just come out once; they are repeatedly forced to come out each and every time they enter a new context, in some cases forcing them to evaluate and re-evaluate every single day the safety of the context in which they are working.

Along the same lines, Guittar (2014:125 emphasis in original) argues:

> *Coming out as a gradual process* and *coming out as a career* are similar in that they both recognize coming out as an ongoing progression. However, there is a sharp distinction between these two conceptions of coming out: a process is eventually completed, while a career is not completed, per se—it is merely managed.

While psychological stage models of coming out, such as Coleman's (1982) developmental stages of the coming out process, propose a linear progression and were a helpful starting place for understanding gender and sexual development, research has shown that coming out is much more complicated than first described (Guittar 2014).

"*Coming out is a function of oppression.* Those groups which enjoy positions of privilege in society rarely, if ever, have to analyze, question, disclose or justify the characteristics of their dominant traits," writes Guittar (2014:4 emphasis in original). Research on coming out often focuses on the process of telling others about one's sexuality or gender identity; however, a key aspect of coming out involves acknowledging this identity to oneself. It is an acknowledgment that your sexuality or gender identity differs from what others expect. In his study of LGBTQ people, Guittar (2014:27) shows, "Self-acceptance is quite central to coming out and not merely a prerequisite." Similarly, Nicolazzo (2017:1) finds that the process of trans people uncovering "our trans* becomings" is a lifelong career.

Whether or not to come out in the classroom, or school more generally, is an important decision that educators must grapple with. One major part of this decision is the school's culture around LGBTQ issues. Coming out should always be an individual's decision, but scholarship has pointed to the benefits for teachers and students when teachers are out in the classroom. Dellenty (2019:100) argues, "The energy many LGBT+ educators are forced to expend in concealment would be better spent on teaching young people." Additionally,

> If school leaders expect fellow professionals to lie about core aspects of themselves in order to keep the peace, young LGBT+ people are being denied openly LGBT+ role models, who could make a positive impact upon young people purely by being their authentic selves at work.
> (Dellenty 2019:100–101)

It is important to be able to see, notice, and recognize all the various gender and sexual presentations around us; it is hard to know of all the possibilities, without visual aids. In this way, Dellenty (2019:101 emphasis ours) concludes, "We all deserve to bring our whole selves to work (*should we choose to*), as do our young people, and it is for us to model our core standards in all we do."

When LGBTQ teachers are out in the classroom, it is also another way to add diverse voices to the curriculum. While the incidence of teachers being out in the classroom varies greatly by grade level, region of the country, and school politics, we advocate for teachers to be as open, and as authentic as possible with students when it is safe for them. The reason for this is that students need to see a variety of gender and sexual identities in the adults that surround them. They need role models, regardless of their gender and sexuality, that present them with diverse and empowered gender and sexual identities.

For illustration, one of the authors of this textbook, Baker, is visibly and openly queer in the classroom and on campus. They believe that being true to themselves allows them to provide a role model for queer students to look up to. This means that they do not hide their personal identities and the status of their relationships, and when appropriate, they use their identities and family as examples in the classroom. For many students, even at the college level, this is the first time they have interacted with a person who is visibly queer and comfortable with their identity. Marni, an open cisgender lesbian, who is also married to a cisgender woman and has two children, is also open in the classroom and has had several students articulate that she is the first openly gay person, never mind educator, they have met. We find, by being ourselves, Baker and Marni encourage acceptance, understanding, and empathy toward gender and sexual minorities.

This is not to say that all teachers need to be out in this specific way; rather, it is to clarify the importance of modeling diversity for our students. Many teachers, especially those who teach younger children, do not feel safe coming out at school.

They still face the potential of harassment and discrimination. Other teachers prefer to keep their professional identities separate from their gender and sexual identities. In *School's Out: Gay and Lesbian Teachers in the Classroom*, Catherine Connell (2015:66) writes about Cheryl, a teacher who prefers not to "mix my sexual orientation with my career." Cheryl's response is not uncommon among teachers who see their sexuality as personal and not relevant to their identities as teachers.

Philip McAdoo (2019:4) explains in the opening of his book, *Independent Queers*, "Being a teacher, I was reluctant to come out…. My experience of school cultures was that of traditional gender norms, heteronormativity, and homophobia… I assumed sharing my identity would distract students from learning." On the contrary, McAdoo found that students benefit when teachers are out. These teachers provide important role models for LGBTQ students and all students. McAddo (2019) recounts his "Proudest Pride Moment" as the time he received a note from a former student thanking him for being "an important role model" for him. "I only came out as gay a few years ago but having you at the school was so important and I really have loved following your career ever since. Hope as is well and happy pride 🏳️‍🌈"—Former Student.

Connell (2015) discusses the experiences of gay and lesbian teachers and demonstrates how they are subject to two conflicting identities: professional and gay. These two identities are not mutually exclusive, or equally supported by schools, and often lead LGBTQ teachers to feel conflicted about what it means to be a professional and what it means to be a member of the LGBTQ community. It also becomes evident that sexual identity in school settings shapes and influences the way one presents and performs their gender (Connell 2015; McAdoo 2019). This matters because how teachers manage their identities influence students' engagement and success in the classroom.

If schools can expand and normalize notions of gender and sexuality beyond the binary, teachers will be less compartmentalized in the classroom. Allowing teachers to be present as their whole selves positively impacts students. For illustration, Connell (2015) introduces Mark, a teacher who struggled with negotiating his gay identity with his professional teacher identity and, for many years, kept his gay identity hidden and closeted. One of his students spotted him at a gay pride parade, and this outing prompted him to rethink how to be both gay and a teacher. Mark's movement from the concealment of his identity as gay to the integration of his gay and teacher identities shows the importance of schools providing space for teachers, students, and administrators to feel safe to "come out."

The gender and sexuality of K-12 educators can have a substantial impact on the way students view and understand their own gender and sexuality. In a brief survey of college students enrolled in a course about gender, Tawanna, a Black cisgender heterosexual woman, explained how the gender and sexuality of their K-12 teachers influenced the way they saw and understood their own gender. For Tawanna, the way her teachers dressed in high school impacted how the dress code rules were enacted in the classroom. Tawanna stated that when her teachers loosened the gender rules in the classroom by being more willing to express their own genders, it helped with her own self-expression and how she handled the pressure to conform to school-wide dress code policies. Overall, when teachers model gender and sexual inclusivity in the classroom, it has a positive impact on students and can lead to a reduction in bullying, harassment, and isolation (Craig and Smith 2014; D'Augelli, Pilkington, and Hershberger 2002; Garner and Emano 2013).

Parent–Teacher Interactions

Having conversations with parents about gender, sexuality, and LGBTQ inclusion is an important part of creating an inclusive culture. Inclusive programs must treat families as partners in the education and care of students (Pastel et al. 2019). This means that teachers must understand that "parents and guardians are their children's first and most important teachers" and teachers must work to "build respectful and strength-based partnerships with families" (Pastel et al. 2019:16). As Pastel et al. (2019:17 *emphasis in original*) explain, "Creating gender inclusive environments takes everyone's participation: that's what *inclusive* means!"

Oftentimes, parents avoid talking with their children about LGBTQ issues simply because they lack confidence and knowledge in this area (Dellenty 2019). As teachers and administrators, you can change this by sending home information, providing educational opportunities, or talking to parents about these issues in conferences. As Pastel et al. (2019:20) describe, "Fear can be a normal experience when approaching new information" and so can discomfort. When someone thinks they understand a topic, like gender and sexuality, and then they find out maybe they are wrong or that other people understand it differently, this can cause them to shut down. If a parent or teacher realizes that something they have been doing may have been harmful to a child, "this could evoke discomfort and a range of feelings including defensiveness, anger, embarrassment, shame, disbelief, and confusion" (Pastel et al. 2019:21).

The goal is to provide the information in ways that parents are open to receiving. We can give them the tools to remedy mistakes they may have made moving forward. We must help parents understand, "It is impossible to grow up surrounded by the 'gender binary' smog, without being deeply affected in ways that consciously and unconsciously influence our attitudes and actions" (Pastel et al. 2019:23). We all hold biases, but we can all work together to overcome them, and it is vital that we do. Parents, like teachers, grapple with learning to support their gender and sexually diverse children, whom they deeply love, yet recognize will grow up in a society that may stigmatize them.

What children learn about gender and sexuality within their families will influence their understandings throughout their lives and their own gender and sexual identities. Thus, it is vital for teachers to be prepared to help parents understand the messages they are sending their children both implicitly and explicitly. Family support has major implications for students' understanding of gender and sexual identities and for their mental health (Pastel et al. 2019). For instance, the 2016 National Center for Transgender Equality (NCTE) survey found that trans respondents who reported unsupportive families had an attempted suicide rate of 54 percent (James et al. 2016). For trans respondents with supportive families, this rate dropped to 37 percent (James et al. 2016); which is clearly better, but still extremely problematic. For reference, the attempted suicide rate for the general population in the United States is 4.6 percent. This data is especially important for teachers and parents of students in K-12 education because 34 percent of respondents report that their first suicide attempt occurred before the age of 14 (James et al. 2016). As these statistics demonstrate, "Parents, families, and teachers have little control over their children's gender identity, but extensive influence over their children's gender health, gender expressions and feelings of affirmation" (Ehrensaft 2016).

Conclusion

When we challenge ourselves to use gender-aware critical pedagogy, we call into question many of the ways we were socialized into binary understandings of gender. We know that the binary approach to gender does not capture many of our students' lived experiences, can be discriminatory, and leads to isolation. Therefore, in this chapter, we have offered a new approach and way of thinking about interactions in the classroom. In the next chapter, we provide a framework of gender-aware critical pedagogy to help teachers and administrators ensure that classrooms and schools are safe for all students.

4
The Application of Gender-Aware Critical Pedagogy

In this chapter, we provide practical guidance on how educators can practice a gender-aware critical approach that centers the needs of students. Our goal is to demonstrate ways teachers can affirm, validate, and empower students' gender and sexual identities while also creating safe and welcoming learning spaces. The gender-aware critical approach we present in this chapter is informed by various existing theories and strategies, including, but not limited to, critical pedagogy, feminist pedagogy, engaged pedagogy, and trauma-informed pedagogy. To fully understand gender-aware critical pedagogy, it is important to begin by discussing the pedagogical strategies that inform its theoretical background.

Paulo Freire (1921–1997), a founder and advocate of critical pedagogy, viewed education as a practice of freedom. He believed that human beings have the inherent potential to transform their world through a process of reflection and action, skills learned via education (Freire 1968). Freire (1968) writes, "The solution is not to 'integrate' them into the structure of oppression, but to transform that structure so that they can become 'beings for themselves.'" For Freire, there is no such thing as "neutral" education. Education either serves as an instrument of conformity or an instrument of freedom. Freire developed a generative method that invited his students' life experiences into his classroom. He used their stories to launch critical academic inquiries into the structures of society.

Building on critical pedagogy, bell hooks (1994) and other feminists began to define the goals of feminist and engaged pedagogies. Feminist and engaged pedagogies attempt to relate course materials to students' everyday lives by "bringing the abstract, historical, or fictional out of the ivory tower and into their own backyards thus making the content more meaningful" (Chick and Hassel 2009:209). Feminists, simply put, are concerned with equally and equitably representing women and other gendered experiences. Some describe feminism as an opportunity to recenter the subject and expand which stories get told.

Relatedly, engaged pedagogies encourage teachers to consider how students make sense of material. Students are much more likely to retain information, and more importantly to think about it critically, when they can see how it relates to their own lives. Therefore, pedagogical strategies that encourage teachers to relate subject area content to students' lived experiences goes a long way in helping students understand and remember important information. Thus, inclusive learning communities synthesize multiple perspectives into a rich tapestry of innovative thoughts and creative ideas.

Critical and feminist educators transform their pedagogical practice to address the needs of students and engage their consciousness in solving real-world problems. Their aim is to empower students to think for themselves, to learn what they most need to know, and to act in their own interests and in the interests of others through acts of solidarity. Based on key tenets of critical inquiry, gender-aware critical pedagogy focuses on the *process* by which learning occurs rather than the acquisition of *content*. When a classroom becomes a shared learning community, students generate rather than consume knowledge. They come to understand that knowledge itself is a social, political, cultural, and historical construct, always value-laden, and always imbued with power (Apple 2019; Sturrock 1979; Wortham 2006). According to Clifford and Marinucci (2008), knowledge is not fixed and static, but an ever-evolving construct built by a community of learners:

> Genuine inquiries demand that understanding develops in a public space in which each person's abilities, interests, perspectives, and talents help move everyone else's thinking forward. It is a knowledge-building space in which ideas are at the center, and each individual has a commitment to producing the collective, evolving understanding.

By presenting the gender binary as a social, historical, and hierarchical construct, the tenets of "knowledge" belying gender bias, stereotypes, and disparities are brought into question. This method calls for an examination of power and inequality. Therefore, a gender-aware critical pedagogy makes the hierarchical ranking system implicit in the gender binary visible and provides students with the opportunity to analyze it as a power structure.

Teaching thus requires building learning communities in which students are involved as knowledge-builders and co-creators. Teaching in this way can help students open their eyes to the world in new ways and grow as both students and citizens. We can motivate students to engage in a lifetime of learning, one that continues long after they leave our classrooms. Only by teaching students *how* to learn can we empower them to also be advocates for social justice and a better world. Wortham (2006) reminds us that social identification and academic learning are inextricably bound, so strengthening students' personal and collective identities strengthens their capacity to learn. When their lives are the subject of study, a sense of interrelatedness in the classroom transfers to greater engagement and motivation to learn (Baxter-Magolda 1999; Freire 1970; Shor 1992; Wink 2011).

Côté and Levine (2002, 2016) define agency as intentional action for the purpose of altering the social environment. Individuals with greater agency have the capacity to resist or act back on coercive social structures that impinge on their identities. Agency is associated with self-esteem, a sense of purpose in life, and increased capacity for self-determination. Because the development of agency always occurs within the uneven power relationships of social systems like race and gender, it is not just a personal process but has systemic implications.

Many students, and some of parents too, have internalized the assumption of a gender binary so thoroughly that it has become implicit in their consciousness, and they have difficulty resisting its influence, even when such ideas cause them harm. Gender-aware critical educators present perspectives that challenge the status quo and encourage the analysis of power relations. A process of critical inquiry empowers students' agency by providing opportunities for reflection, social interaction, communal knowledge-building, and forums for action.

Trauma-Informed Pedagogy

Trauma-informed pedagogy "requires having a keen awareness of our students' past and present experiences and the effects of those experiences on students' well-being" (Imad 2020). To ensure that all students feel safe and empowered in the classroom, teachers must recognize that students with marginalized gender and sexual identities may have experiences of trauma. Because trauma affects a person's ability to complete basic tasks by impairing concentration, decision-making, and connecting with others, teachers must be aware of how trauma may be affecting their students.

Imad (2020), a neuroscientist and expert on teaching and learning, provides several basic tips to assist teachers in taking trauma seriously when developing our pedagogy.

- Teachers must ensure that students feel safe emotionally, cognitively, physically, and interpersonally in our classrooms. When students do not feel safe, it is difficult, or impossible, to learn. The brain prioritizes our safety over learning, and therefore, the ability to take in new information is hampered if a student feels unsafe.
- Teachers should strive to foster an environment of trust and transparency. To do this, teachers must connect and communicate with students. By being clear, transparent, and reliable, teachers build trust with their students. In addition to building trust and healthy relationships with your students, teachers can facilitate building relationships between students. Teaching students to care for one another is a lesson that will help them throughout their lives because it allows them to cultivate and express empathy.
- Teachers should promote collaboration and mutuality by sharing power and decision-making in the classroom. Obviously, students' ages and abilities will influence how this is carried out, but all classrooms can benefit from collaboration. Working with students in partnership will teach them lifelong lessons that go beyond the traditional banking model of education (Freire 1970). In the traditional banking model of education, the teachers' sole role is to transmit content knowledge to their students. They "deposit" information into their students' minds, and students passively receive the information they transmit. Later, the teacher makes a "withdrawal," asking students to regurgitate the information, usually in the form of a test. Critical educators use a more generative approach by including students' voices in the curriculum and building shared knowledge among a community of learners. When appropriate, they ask students to voice their opinions or have them co-create assignments and projects. To feel empowered, students need some degree of authority. Furthermore, creating an environment of mutuality

means that if students are not in a place to learn, they will feel safe and comfortable sharing this with you.

Imad (2020) encourages educators to "empower voice and choice by identifying and helping build on student strengths." Validating and normalizing students' concerns and fears helps them build confidence and agency. Children must learn how to advocate for themselves and others. Finally, stress the importance of having a sense of purpose which provides students with hope and meaning.

Framework for a Gender-Aware Critical Pedagogy

Developing a gender-aware critical pedagogical approach shares common themes with other critical approaches to learning. We offer seven areas of development that build professional competencies for gender-aware critical educators.

1. Start with Yourself

First and foremost, it is imperative that we, as educators, understand the influence our own social positions have on our students. This self-inquiry involves examining the ways our attitudes have been shaped by our upbringing and educational backgrounds. Building cultural competency is a lifetime commitment, and educators must understand the impact social identities, our own and those of our students, have on both teaching and learning. This includes exploring the history and current environment of our subject areas through an equity lens. It involves deepening a pedagogy that challenges the status quo and encourages critical thinking and systems learning.

Without personal awareness, no amount of teacher education will be sufficient for providing all students with an equitable education experience. As Ortiz and Patton (2012:10) explain, "To practice inclusion, individual professionals need to conduct a profound exploration of their personal values and beliefs as well as understand how they enter into their work with students and institutions." Ortiz and Patton (2012:11) believe that "understanding one's own... worldview is the starting place for understanding others." Educators must be willing to examine their values and assumptions and be aware of how their own attitudes and behaviors affect their students.

In *Intersectionality in Action: A Guide for Faculty and Campus Leaders for Creating Inclusive Classrooms and Institutions*, Niki Latino (2016:31–32) provides a list of "Best Practices and Action Steps" for becoming an inclusive leader. They emphasize the importance of understanding your own personal story. We tell stories in daily conversations, and our stories shape our truth and our reality. They encourage a continuous process of questioning. How and why do we assign labels based on biases? How can we learn to listen to how people identify themselves rather than assigning identities?

Latino (2016) cautions against using guilt as an excuse to avoid exploring the construction of privileged identities and one's own personal privilege. Each of us as an individual is not responsible for changing history; however, we have a shared responsibility to transform present and future contexts. We can allow our transformative life experiences to be doors and windows into greater and deeper understanding by intentionally engaging in critical discourse and self-reflexivity about these experiences.

One practical way teachers can equip themselves for dealing with issues of gender and sexuality is to prepare answers for questions that may arise (Key 2014). People are inquisitive, especially children; therefore, by preparing for questions that may come up from students and parents, such as questions about where a particular student uses the restroom, you can be ready to provide knowledge and be confident in what you say. By being prepared, you are more likely to be confident in your responses and know that you are doing what is in the best interest of your students.

2. Cultivate Compassion and Respond with Empathy

Because identity is so complex and intersectional, educators must have empathy and be willing to continue learning to create inclusive classrooms and school environments. Empathy is the willingness and ability to take the perspective of someone else. Educators must step outside of themselves and try to understand situations from the point of view of students who experience the world differently than themselves. As educators, fortunately, most of us already strive to engage and support our students; we are highly empathetic, open, and curious about our students and their lives.

An important aspect of learning and practicing empathy is being open to hearing other people's perspectives on an issue or situation. Ortiz and Patton (2012:23) remind us that in these sometimes-difficult conversations, it is "helpful to remember basic, good communication skills such as the use of 'I' statements and a readiness to admit to misunderstandings."

FIGURE 4.1
Source: Anastasiia Makarevich

For illustration, consider that a student yells out that the book his teacher just read aloud to the class, *Heather has Two Mommies*, is gross. How should his teacher handle this situation? She could reprimand him for yelling. She could get offended and tell the student he is wrong. Or, she could try to understand his perspective, while also acknowledging that there is a student in the class who has two mommies. She could start by saying:

> Chad, I appreciate that you have thoughts on the book we are reading, and I would like to hear them, but I'm not sure I understand why you think the book is gross. I like this book and think it is a good story about family. Could you tell me why you think it's gross?

Maybe, Chad responds, "Because people kiss in it and kissing is gross." Maybe he didn't care that the book was about two mommies; rather, he was grossed out by kissing because he is five years old. On the other hand, maybe Chad says it's gross because his church tells him that families are made up of a mommy and a daddy, not two mommies. Now that the teacher understands Chad's perspective and has validated his ability to share his perspective, she can use his comment as a teaching moment. She can explain that while people may have different beliefs, in this class, we celebrate all types of loving families, and even when we don't agree, we can still show respect because many of the students in the class have different types of families.

To use these experiences as teaching moments rather than shut down our students, we must respond from a place of empathy.

The first step in cultivating empathy is to develop self-awareness and understanding of ourselves and our own views. Ortiz and Patton (2012:25) provide a list of key steps for gaining more self-awareness and "developing an inclusive disposition."

- ◆ Honestly evaluate your current beliefs and attitudes. Think about where your ideas and beliefs about social

issues have come from; what is the history of your information, and how has this shaped your worldview.
- Be willing to take risks. At times, you may feel vulnerable, but vulnerability is part of learning and is not a bad thing if we embrace it and have the courage to express it.
- Create a safe space conducive to introspection, what hooks (1990) calls a "homeplace," where it is okay to make mistakes and work through setbacks with other people you trust. We discuss this step more in area 7.

3. Take an Intersectional Approach

Collins and Bilge (2016:25) describe intersectionality as "a way of understanding and analyzing the complexity of the world, in people, and in human experience." The term "intersectionality" refers to overlapping aspects of identity and overlapping systems of oppression (Crenshaw 2016). No one is just their gender, their race, or their sexuality. Identity is more complex than a single aspect and instead consists of multiple intersecting components. For example, what it means to be a young Black gay man is different from what it means to be a young white gay man. Race and many other identities intersect with our gender and sexuality to create unique and complex experiences for everyone.

FIGURE 4.2
Source: wildpixel

Intersectionality, as a way of thinking, helps us to consider how our various identities interlock with one another to locate us in a diverse and multifaceted society. Intersectionality also demonstrates how our identities position our ability to access resources, such as cultural capital. White women, for example, are members of a privileged race, but are subject to sexism. Men of color inevitably face racism but some may be oblivious to sexism. Women of color experience both racism and sexism. Lesbian and trans women of color face the intersection of race, gender, and sexuality oppression. Arab Muslims encounter both racial and religious discrimination. Because all of our identities intertwine in the lives of every individual, Collins (1990, 2016) argues that racism, classism, sexism, and other forms of oppression are inextricably bound.

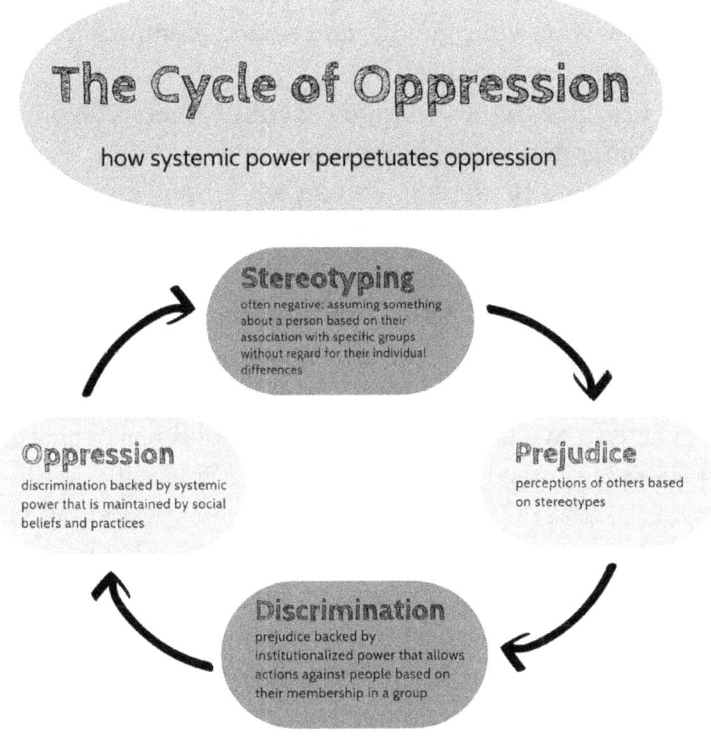

FIGURE 4.3
Source: Infographic by Alex J. Mack

As teachers, our job is to invite the multiple aspects of our students' identities into our classrooms and to provide opportunities for them to share their authentic selves and learn more about the experiences of others. As gender-aware educators, we want to recognize students' gender and sexual identities as primary aspects of their identity, but also recognize that they are so much more than just their gender and sexual identities. Our approach also needs to recognize race, social class, family and cultural backgrounds, as well as, emotional temperaments, learning styles, linguistic codes, and all the other aspects that make up the complex constellations of who they are.

Think about the intersecting identities in your own constellation.

- How have your gender and sexual identities influenced your worldview and sense of reality?
- How were your gender and sexual identities influenced by your upbringing?
- How does your religious identity intersect with your gender and sexual identities?
- In what situations have you felt empowered or disempowered by your gender and sexual identities?

Exploring the intersections of your own identity in relationship to what Collin's calls "interlocking systems of oppression" can help you relate to the multidimensional identities of your students.

An activity we use with both students and teachers is called "Ten Aspects of My Identity." We've used this with children as young as seven and with C-Suite executives. We ask the participants to list ten aspects of their identities, groups that they belong to, or characteristics that define who they are. For instance, nine-year-old Travis listed aspects of his identity as mixed-race, boy, smart, athletic, son, brother, and a gamer. Seven-year-old Shaun listed artist, reader, rock climber, and singer. Everyone's identity is a constellation of many aspects, and these various categories of being all form the story of who we are as unique individuals.

Next, we invite the participants to identify three core aspects of who they are and create a pie chart that shows how important each of the three aspects are in their lives. Then they work in small groups to share the story of their pie. They discuss questions, such as, why are each of those aspects of identity meaningful to you? Or, who or what has influenced these parts of your identities? Activities like these help all students better understand themselves and understand how identity unfolds in a reciprocal relationship with their environments.

It is especially important to expose young women of color to narratives that affirm their perspectives of their race, gender, and other aspects of their identities (Caldwell and Frame 2022). Here are two examples of learning experiences that can help students understand these intersecting identities.

- In a literature class reading Adichie's (2012) *Purple Hibiscus*, the main character, Kambili, is influenced by the legacy of colonialism in Nigeria. Her race, gender, social status, and religious identities all intersect and are crucial to understanding how her story plays out.
- In a history class, students might be studying feminism and the women's suffrage movements, but part of this struggle involved power dynamics between Black, Latina, Asian, Indigenous, and white women. Likewise, the political dynamics between cisgender heterosexual women and women with diverse gender and sexual identities not only have historical roots but are an important part of the current debate in feminism. An intersectional focus allows students to understand that power and disempowerment play out in different ways for different groups.

Taking an intersectional approach means making sure that none of our students' multiple identities are taboo (Frame 2021). When we include diverse voices in conversations in our classrooms, we reach deeper understandings of the ways people in our communities exist, and these conversations create truly dynamic, eye-opening learning experiences. The future of learning is an equal and inclusive space where students can open up and be vulnerable. They can bring their whole selves into the classroom and not check parts of themselves at the door (Caldwell and Frame 2022).

Imad (2020) also recommends keeping intersectionality in the forefront of your mind when working with students who have experienced trauma. Acknowledge that students may have different kinds of traumas, and individual students may need to deal with these traumas differently. Having empathy and seeing students' intersecting identities will help teachers not to re-traumatize students.

As teachers, the way we see our students impacts how they see themselves, how they relate to school, and how well they learn. By creating classroom environments that affirm multiple aspects of their identities, we can ensure that we provide mirrors that reflect back the most promising picture of their emerging self.

4. Create an Identity-Safe and Brave Learning Community

Equity frameworks and culturally relevant pedagogies emphasize the necessity of building an identity-safe and brave learning community. Before engaging in conversations about gender identity, expression, and sexual identity, clear communication guidelines must be in place. An identity-safe environment invites students' stories into the classroom and welcomes their emotional expressions about experiences with power and marginalization. An identity-brave environment frames vulnerability as courage, encourages "leaning into the discomfort," and allows grace for making mistakes.

To create an identity-safe and brave space, educators must teach and highly recommend respectful communication skills that foster relationships; teach students to listen with compassion and respond with empathy; provide instruction on emotional and social literacy; and reward students for their emotional labor and acts of compassion as well as for their intellectual labor. Remember that students want nothing more than to belong. If you can create belongingness in your classroom, the quality and speed of learning will dramatically increase. The empathy you cultivate among your students will allow their thinking to expand and their perspectives to broaden.

Janene, a high school journalism teacher, taught classes virtually during the pandemic. Students in her school could choose whether they attended in person or virtually, and Janene's students chose to attend virtually. Schoolwide absenteeism was a problem, but especially among the virtual learners. Janene was concerned that her students were disengaged and isolated, so she redesigned her curriculum to better engage their interests. When she invited them to share their experiences about their race, gender, and social class identities, they responded immediately. Janene saw that they were making social connections and building relationships. She realized that they were hungry for these kinds of interactions because they were learning more about each other's lives, and she knew of course, that high school students thrive on peer relationships.

One day during class, Janene noticed that Avery had added the pronouns "they/them" to their screen name. When another student asked them about it, Avery explained that they identified as nonbinary. Some of the students didn't know what that meant, so Avery explained that they don't consider themselves to have a binary gender identity that is either a boy or a girl. Avery's story opened the door for other students to talk about their own gender experiences, and by the end of the week, three more students had added *chosen names* and *pronouns* to their screen names.

As her students revealed more about their sense of gender identity and their experience at school, Janene realized that these kids weren't attending school in person because they were hiding. They were afraid to go to school because they had been judged, excluded, ridiculed, and harassed. During one class, Sarita shared, "I'm Black and gay and my family doesn't have much money, so I've always felt like an outsider, but when you find other outsiders, you're not an outsider anymore." Because Janene created a space safe for them to share their stories, these students found out they weren't alone. In Janene's class, they were "normal." When they returned to campus the next semester, they knew that they had an adult advocate and a supportive community.

5. Represent Diverse Voices and Perspectives

Sara Bloomberg and Terri Hennessy (2020), Montessori teachers who work closely with gender and sexuality educators, choose books that represent a diversity of gender identities and gender-related themes to start conversations with their young students. Sara stated,

> I may read a book about a boy who likes to wear dresses and ask one question. I might ask, 'Who says a boy can't wear a dress?' and that one question leads to a lively discussion. Questions prompt critical thinking.

Students need to see themselves represented in their classrooms and school. Therefore, it is imperative to represent gender-diverse and intersectional identities on the walls, in the halls, and in all academic materials.

Students also need to be exposed to counter-narratives that challenge the gender binary, the gender hierarchy, and patriarchy. They need to know about the contributions of LGBTQ activists, scientists, and authors. They need to read books with LGBTQ characters and themes. They need to be introduced to unsung heroes whose contributions have been invisible in traditional curricula. The works of queer authors of color can be revolutionary in the depth of thinking they present, such as James Baldwin, Ocean Vuong, Jesmyn Ward, Gloria Anzaldua, and Audre Lorde, to name but a few. The story of Bayard Rustin, a gay man and organizing force behind the March on Washington, presents a thoughtful exploration of intersections of race, class, gender, and sexual identities. Or the story of Marsha P. Johnson, queer activist and drag queen, can demonstrate how queer people have always been involved in movements for liberation. From understanding terminology to understanding LGBTQ histories and herstories, students need to know that gender and sexually diverse people have always been involved in the struggle for equality.

Information, resources, and support for curricula development can be found on the websites of the Gay and Lesbian Alliance against Defamation (GLAAD 2021), Gay, Lesbian and Straight Education Network (GLSEN 2021), Human Rights Campaign (HRC 2021), Parents, Families and Friends of Lesbians and Gays (PFLAG 2021), and Gender Spectrum (2019).

LGBTQ histories and herstories tell stories that have been hidden but not erased. Erin, a middle school teacher, uses project-based inquiries to steer inquiries into LGBTQ history. "Kids know about Stonewall," she says. "And yes, that was a watershed event, but LGBTQ history didn't start or end there." She uses *A Queer History of the United States for Young People* (Chevat and Bronski 2019) as a resource. Mark teaches a course called Perspectives on Gender Diversity. His students started an archive for LGBTQ history in their school and conducted oral interviews with teachers, students, and alumni. Oman invites a group of LGBTQ adults to sit on a panel in his sociology class. They answer students' questions about how they came out to their families and how they negotiate gender and sexual identities in their daily lives. By engaging with this panel, students gain a new depth of understanding. Their comments reveal that for some of them, this is the first time they have realized that sexuality and identity are dimensions of love.

6. Provide Emotionally and Academically Rigorous Curriculum

Many equity frameworks emphasize the importance of academically "rigorous" curricula. However, in our experience, the calls for "rigor" and "grit" have typically been aimed at girls and students of color. All too often, the emphasis on rigor reinforces the deficit narrative by upholding dominant culture norms as the standard for academic excellence. Gender-aware pedagogy emphasizes the role of *emotional* rigor, which we believe challenges the gender binary and the patriarchy by bringing into question the norms of schooling as an academic experience devoid of feeling.

While your job as a K-12 educator is not to provide mental health care for children, there are some skills you can teach all children to help them succeed in life. One skill that is vital for all students to learn is emotional resilience. Emotional resilience "is critical to build healthy coping skills" (Flores and Day 2006; Rodgers and Scott 2008; Sachs 2005). All students, but especially gender and sexually diverse students, benefit from building emotional resiliency and coping skills. For example, you can ask students to share how they cope with stress, so they can learn coping strategies from each other. So often students cope with stress in creative ways—through poetry, music, art, drama, and creating video content—and when invited to share their creations, they are most happy to do so. You can ask them about their support systems—who do they turn to when they are struggling? What helps? What inspires them? How do they take care of themselves?

You can provide instruction on gender microaggressions, introducing a few common scenarios, and then asking if anyone would like to share examples from their own lives. Collectively, they can generate potential responses to such scenarios. You can help students strengthen personal boundaries by inviting them to discuss possible answers to inappropriate questions they may be asked about their gender and sexuality. If such questions come from adults, the student may suggest that the adult could speak to their parents instead of them. If they come from other students, they can respond with "That's personal," or "That's inappropriate," or "I don't feel comfortable answering that question."

By participating in these conversations in the classroom, they gain necessary skills and peer support to protect themselves from invasive questions and assaultive comments. These conversations also cultivate language for their classmates who want to intervene as allies and advocates. In Martha's eighth-grade classroom, her students brainstormed ways to "interrupt" gender oppression in non-confrontational ways. Scott reported a few days later that when the boys on his baseball team used terms like "gay" and "fag," he felt powerful when he said, "That's not cool, guys, cut it out."

When students explore their felt experience, learn to attune to and process their emotions, and connect what they are learning in school to their lives outside of school, they believe that what they are learning matters. As a result, their motivation increases, and they are inspired to work hard to accomplish their own learning goals. This kind of rigor is a byproduct of emotional *and* academic inquiry and supports them in developing agency.

7. Cultivate Your Educator's Support Network

We strongly recommend that gender and sexuality educators join or create a group in which they can find support for this important work. In a group of like-minded educators who share a passion for justice, educators can find the support and encouragement they need to sustain their work. We need people who share our passions and who we can count on to encourage our own transformational growth. We stress the imperative need for educators who are leading the way in gender-inclusive education work to intentionally build networks of connections. It is essential to have a judgment-free zone with trusted allies to process our feelings and thoughts (Ortiz and Patton 2012). Establishing an inclusion and equality group with other teachers and administrators at your school is a good place to start. No one can do this work alone. If you don't already have a network of educators who share your commitment to gender justice, we encourage you to start building one today. If you need support and it's not available in your school, we invite you to join iChange Collaborative's LGBTQ Resource Group for Educators.

We must create spaces in our lives for challenging discourse. Too often, political correctness is used as an excuse to not engage in difficult dialogue. Engaging in respectful, honest dialogue is critical to developing inclusive leadership. Using the dialogic method for our own growth and transformation will continue to empower our work.

Conclusion

These tenets of gender-aware critical pedagogy challenge both the explicit and the hidden curriculum of schooling and offer guidance for transformational education on both personal and systemic levels. As Latino (2016) reminds us, we cannot afford to take breaks from working toward inclusive excellence. Our students who are not part of the dominant group cannot take breaks, and when others do, it leaves them to shoulder the responsibility. Once we understand our students' deep need for acceptance, affirmation, validation, and empowerment, taking a break is no longer an option.

That being said, self-care is important for anyone doing diversity and inclusion work, no matter what their identity or social location. This work is a marathon, not a sprint, and we need to make sure we are prepared for the long game. Burnout is real, and developing mechanisms and support systems for self-protection, healthy boundaries, and self-compassion are imperative.

Developing competency as a gender-inclusive educator requires a commitment to continuing education and professional growth. It means reexamining messages that shaped your initial understandings of privilege and your personal identities. This type of self-reflection can be explored through conversations with colleagues, reading social media posts, journaling, commenting on one's own and others' biases and assumptions about gender and sexuality, and narrating your story in various professional arenas. We often need mirrors to help us understand how we participate in a hierarchical binary system of gender that is often implicit in our thinking as we move through our lives in predominantly cisgender and heterosexual environments.

We will make mistakes but learning from mistakes inspires continued personal growth and development. We are all works in progress trying to grow and develop on this challenging journey together.

5

Institutional Experiences of Gender and Sexuality

Policies, Programs, and Plans

In this chapter, we discuss how to make education as a social institution more welcoming and inclusive for all students. This chapter takes an institutional view and discusses schooling as a primary institution of socialization; one that embeds a hierarchical gender binary in several ways. Schools regulate gender and sexual identity and expression through curriculum, dress codes, classroom activities, and access to extracurricular activities such as clubs and sports. We examine how policies, programs, and plans can support gender and sexual inclusivity in both the classroom and in the larger school setting. We explore controversies surrounding Title IX, sex education, bathroom access for transgender and nonbinary students, the importance of addressing gender bullying, and providing safe zones and affinity spaces for LGBTQ students. We look at diversity, equity, and inclusion statements, as well as plans, programs, and policies that have worked to support inclusivity and a sense of belonging. Throughout the chapter, we provide examples of teachers and schools who are responding with practices that make their entire schools more inclusive. Jack, a 47-year-old white, cisgender, heterosexual, first-grade teacher, shares how he addresses gender and sexuality in his classroom. He explains that in the years he's been teaching, his understanding of gender and sexuality has evolved considerably:

> I have worked hard to be open to develop my understanding of gender and sexuality. The biggest thing I've learned is that it is ok to make mistakes as long as the children and families know that I am committed to providing a safe, loving class for their child.

FIGURE 5.1
Source: LightFieldStudios

Jack sees gender expressions playing out on the playground and in the classroom. He sees boys generally playing more athletic games, while girls typically play in the sandbox and engage in pretend play. Boys play fighting games, and there are often one or two girls who look to join in. He often sees girls and boys involved in tag games together, though it is common for the games to evolve into boys versus girls. Inside, girls are more likely to draw during choice times. Both genders enjoy building with magnet and wooden blocks, though boys are the ones who primarily build with Legos.

Jack believes that the biggest issues teachers face are the boys' versus girls' games. These games create tensions and divisions in his class. To interrupt the gender binary, Jack frequently engages his students in conversations about gender norms. "We often have discussions about what is a 'boy/girl color' or 'boy/girl clothing.'" He introduces topics about gender through "lots and lots of books and class discussions, and these talks continue throughout the year."

Jack's story reflects many teachers' experiences with gender in the classroom, as well as the way children use gender to organize themselves in the context of school. Much of what happens with gender in school settings demonstrates that school and education are organized as social institutions, formal organizations, that express and support ideas of dominant culture, such as the gender binary.

In this chapter, we explore gender, sexuality, and schools as social institutions. We examine the ways dominant or hegemonic ideals of gender and sexuality shape the classroom and school environment. In addition to individual and interactional changes, institutional changes are needed for all students to feel comfortable, safe, and included. Inclusivity and accessibility in schools, or lack thereof, reveal the ways educational experiences are rooted in social and cultural power, and where the need for change lies. Schools are institutions that transmit knowledge and values about social life, including, but not limited to, gender and sexuality. For example, activities, such as "daddy daughter dances," institutionally support heterosexuality and cisnormativity. Or more generally, dances organized around heterosexuality and cisgender identities can lead to struggles for LGBTQ teachers, students, and parents (Connell 2015; McAdoo 2019).

We also discuss different ways policies, programs, and plans can support gender and sexual inclusivity in both the classroom and in the larger school setting. Codifying and institutionalizing ideas to support students, teachers, and staff is very important to the building of a safe school. This chapter reviews sex education curriculum; Title IX policies; policies on bathroom usage; policies on gendered bullying; safe zones and gay/straight alliances; and gender and sexuality diversity statements. We look at diversity, equity, and inclusion statements as well as plans, programs, and policies that have worked to support inclusivity and a sense of belonging.

What Is an Institution?

Institutions are organizations or patterns of social order that are socially constructed and reflect dominant cultural trends of behavior, practice, and thought. Social institutions enable access to social mobility, personal power, and avenues to personal development. Unfortunately, social institutions are not open to all members equally, and barriers get put in place that limit access to certain resources. In our society, institutions are strongly influenced by dominant ideas and systems of oppression, such as patriarchy, heteronormativity, capitalism, and white supremacy (Brown and Dyer-Stewart 2018). For instance, patriarchy (a male-dominated system) and heteronormativity (a system of oppression that places heterosexuality as the norm) often enter schools through events and activities that reinforce the gender and heterosexual binary. This can occur when schools create programs and curriculum that are organized around gender as performed differently by boys and girls. This often leads to boys and girls being separated, and those that do not align with a binary gender are often left out or asked to conform to the current structure.

School is a place for socialization. Whether public or private, education is a central institution in society, and one that individuals engage with across the life course. School, like family, is considered a primary institution in the United States. As such, schools both enable and constrain our lives. Education is key to social mobility. Even though inequity and inequality happen in schools, as members of society we are taught to value school and its promise of social mobility. Education is seen as a key to success, and thus, it is perceived as a necessary institution. But at the same time, schools construct restrictions and boundaries, such as dictating dress code and what classes students take. Education is carefully organized and controlled, dictating the who, what, when, where, and how of teaching and learning. Schools have historically reflected the values of those with culturally dominant identities, such as those who identify as heterosexual, cisgender, and white. This can result in negative consequences, such as teachers and administrators using gender, sexuality, and race as tracking markers to disenfranchise, marginalize, and punish students of color, especially if they identify as a gender or sexual minority (Carter 2005; Morris 2015, 2017; Rio 2017; Tatum 2017).

Gender and Sexuality as Institutions

A gendered institution is one in which gender is an organizing principle. Gender and sexuality are institutionalized within the framework of education and schools, creating and enforcing specific ways of thinking about these constructs. In a gendered institution, boys and girls are channeled into different, and often differently valued, social spaces or activities and their "choices" have different and often unequal consequences (Lorber 1994; Risman 1998). Therefore, there is a need to encourage teachers and administrators in schools that rely on gender and sexuality for social order to reimagine organizational and institutional flow. Let's first think about teachers and the impact their identities have on informal and formal classroom organization and learning.

Sawyer is a seventh-grade science teacher who identifies as gender fluid. Although many of their colleagues know about their gender identity, Sawyer wishes that their colleagues were more knowledgeable about gender and sexuality. They say, "The world is changing, and teachers need to be educated about these issues." Sawyer notices gender differences in their classroom: girls in their science classes are quieter and tend to define their value by the grades they get, while boys are louder, interrupt more, and tend to find more value in their athletic ability than their grades.

Sawyer attempts to intentionally create a culture of inclusion in their classroom. When students use terms like "lesbian," "gay," and "homo" in demeaning ways, Sawyer stops the class to address these comments. Sawyer asks, "What does that word mean to you?" This question opens a discussion that gives students a chance to reflect on the messages they are sending, explore the underlying assumptions such slurs imply, and think about how these words may impact LGBTQ people (and those who love them). Sawyer continues, "I use the same approach if a boy makes a comment about doing 'x' like a girl."

Unfortunately, Sawyer's school doesn't have policies in place to address these kinds of comments and behaviors, so it's left up to individual teachers to intervene, educate, and help students develop healthy attitudes about gender and sexual identities. Sawyer would like collective support from the institution, wishing more of their colleagues would intervene and interrupt sexist and homophobic language. Sawyer's observations, however, reflect the GLSEN school climate survey which reports that students routinely hear transphobic, homophobic, and sexist comments from peers and sometimes even from school staff. Unfortunately, students report that rarely do they see school personnel intervene to stop it (GLSEN 2019).

Sawyer approaches inclusivity in their classroom by representing nonconforming gender identities visually on their classroom walls. For example, they display a poster of Bianca Del Rio, a drag queen, comedian, and actor, on the wall behind their desk. When students ask questions about the poster, Sawyer takes the opportunity to talk about drag culture and share some of their own experiences of not fitting in. Sawyer says, "It's not in the curriculum, but when building relationships with students, it's just another way I educate."

Moving Beyond the Binary

Angela, a first-grade teacher in an independent school, has her students draw self-portraits at the beginning of the year. She lets the kids decide how to present themselves. Last year, Lewis drew himself wearing a dress. Angela said:

> Some students tried to tell him he couldn't do that, but my co-teacher and I intervened, and it was a great teaching moment. His self-portrait, wearing the dress, was up on display all year along with everyone else's. I talked to his mother before we hung it up in case it was a touchy subject. His mother was not surprised and happy to have him depict himself authentically.

Angela's story shows how educators can interact with gender to shape and influence how students see themselves and each other. When gender is seen only as a dichotomy, it promotes the idea that there are two separate and opposite genders that are not equal (West and Zimmerman 1987). Angela was able to expand her young students' notions of gender when some of them responded to Lewis's self-portrait saying that a boy can't wear a dress. She not only created a space of belonging for Lewis, but she helped other students move beyond binary thinking about gender. Angela's story also demonstrates that gender manifests itself in our classrooms despite our beliefs, personalities, and interactions. Even if we reject the gender binary ourselves and refuse to let others police us, gender and gender inequality remain woven into the fabric of our lives.

Schools institutionalize the gender binary in several ways, and each institution has its own values, norms, and statuses. Therefore, the way that gender shapes schools will vary from institution to institution. For example, schools that offer or provide school uniforms might have different gendered concerns with dress codes than schools that feel obligated to monitor individual clothes and outfits. Dress codes for uniforms and individual clothes can be sexist, racist, and classist, but how a school handles such matters will vary. We see this matter particularly when we consider the rules of public versus private or independent schools, which have different and often competing financial resources. Private schools do not receive government funding and thus, can have rules and policies that do not conform to state or federal laws. Some religious or same-sex schools may qualify for exemptions when considering gender and sexuality rules and or codes of conduct (Executive Order on Preventing and Combating Discrimination on the Basis of Gender Identity or Sexual Orientation, 2021, Jan 20; Fact Sheet on U.S. Department of Education Policy on Transgender Students, 2016, Aug 15). Let's now look at some institutional ways gender and sexuality become institutionalized in our policies, programs, and plans.

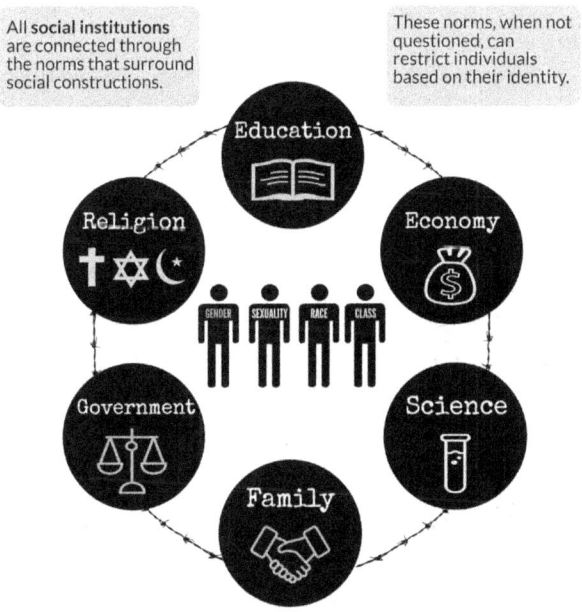

FIGURE 5.2
Source: Infographic by Alex J. Mack

Sex Education

One important example of how schools enforce cis- and heteronormativity is through sex education curriculum. Overall, only 30 states and the District of Columbia mandate that public schools teach sex education at all, and only 17 require program content to be medically accurate (Guttmacher Institute 2020). Schools that offer sex education usually only present information about heterosexual sexual activity. In fact, in many states, teachers are not legally allowed to teach about same-sex relationships during sex education. In sum, 11 states and the District of Columbia require inclusive content about sexuality, while six states require only negative information be provided about same-sex relationships and that a positive emphasis be placed on heterosexuality (Guttmacher Institute 2020). A 2015 survey of Millennials found that only 12 percent of students said that same-sex relationships were covered in their sex education class (Public Religion Research Institute).

Bella, a director at an independent school, believes a comprehensive sex education curriculum helps students better understand gender, sex, and sexuality. This is especially true if sex education can be a component of the K-12 curriculum based on development. For example, students in this educator's elementary school learn about the body, its functions, and how it changes over time. When these students enter middle school, they are exposed to a curriculum that covers sexuality and identity, encouraging students to rely on what they learned about bodies in previous years but to also consider how sexual attraction, curiosity, and attraction begin to occur. The educator emphasized that they spend a lot of time talking about relationships, self-worth, and healthy habits. As these students approach high school, the curriculum begins to take on discussions of consent, sexual activity, protection, and agency. Bella emphasizes that sex education is not a one-size-fits-all curriculum nor is it always helpful to teach or discuss it one time during one class. A truly comprehensive approach brings sex education into the curriculum on a regular basis, with developmentally appropriate information and explanations so students feel empowered to have healthy and happy relationships to their sexual bodies and lives.

Title IX

FIGURE 5.3
Source: utah778

On June 23, 1972, Title IX of the education amendments of 1972 was enacted into law. Title IX prohibits federally funded educational institutions from discriminating against students or employees based on *sex*. It begins: "No person in the United States shall, on the basis of sex, be excluded from participation in, be denied the benefits of, or be subjected to discrimination under any education program or activity receiving Federal financial assistance." As a result of Title IX, any school that receives federal money from the elementary to university level (in short, nearly all schools) must provide fair and equal treatment of the sexes in all areas, including athletics. While Title IX covers much more than sports, here we will focus on this one aspect of the policy.

FIGURE 5.4
Source: monkeybusinessimages

One major goal of Title IX legislation was to correct the limited opportunities for female athletes. Sports have been predominantly played and organized by boys and men. Sport is a patriarchal social institution that continues to favor boys and men as evidenced by the disproportionate resources they receive in schools and professional sports, with football being the clearest example in the United States (Allison 2018; Bridges 2019; Bridges and Pascoe 2014, 2017; Messner 2002). Boys and men continued to receive more funding, be paid more money, and given more attention and media coverage than women in sports (Allison 2018; Pascoe and Bridges 2014).

Institutional Experiences of Gender and Sexuality ◆ 121

FIGURE 5.5
Source: GoodLifeStudio

Sports, like all social institutions, are socially constructed and change as society does. Currently, sports are almost always single-sex or single-gender, and as such, support heterosexuality and cisnormativity. Women, girls, and gender-nonconforming people have been advocating for equal treatment in sports throughout history. Notable voices include Venus Williams, who argued for equal prize money for women and men at Wimbledon; Skylar Diggins-Smith, who advocates for equal pay in professional basketball where men's starting contracts average eight times those of women; and, the U.S. Women's Soccer Team, who are arguing for equal pay as well as equitable medical treatment, training conditions, and coaching (Allison 2018; Petri and Das 2021).

Although the institution of sports is changing, primarily due to gender activists fighting for fair and equal play, the rules and norms around gender continue to organize sports in a way that benefits binary gender performances over others. Sports often negate the participation, and even existence of, gender

FIGURE 5.6
Source: skynesher

nonbinary and intersex athletes. Sport is an institution that is rooted in *gender as difference* (West and Zimmerman 1987) and treats those who do not define themselves within the binary system as outsiders. Due to this, for some time, identifying openly as an LGBTQ athlete has been seen as risky (Pascoe and Bridges 2014).

Since the enactment of Title IX, sports have become more open to diverse experiences and receptive to social change (Allison 2018' Messner 2002; Nicolazzo 2017). Girl's and women's participation in sports has grown exponentially. In high school, the number of girl athletes has increased tenfold from just 295,000 in 1972 to more than 3.3 million in 2015–2016 (NCWGE 2017). In college, the number has grown from 30,000 in 1972 to more than 214,000 in 2015–2016 (NCWGE 2017). In addition, Title IX is credited with decreasing the dropout rate of girls from high school and increasing the number of women who pursue higher education and complete college degrees (NCWGE 2017).

However, as wonderful as Title IX has been for a variety of inclusive measures, historically it has not been utilized to address gender or sexuality. Title IX was designed to prevent discrimination based on sex in and at all levels of education. What exactly "sex" means for discriminatory purposes—and, particularly, a person's transgender status—has not been made clear (Wickliffe 2020). In this way, we know that there are consequences of policies such as Title IX, and our hope is to recognize these flaws to improve the educational lives of all students, regardless of sex, gender, or sexuality.

On June 15, 2020, the U.S. Supreme Court held that discrimination based on an individual's status as gay or transgender constitutes sex discrimination within the meaning of Title VII of the Civil Rights Act of 1964 (See *Bostock v. Clayton Cty.*, Ga., 140 S. Ct. 1731, 1741 (2020). The court stated, "It is impossible to discriminate against a person for being homosexual or transgender without discriminating against that individual based on sex." In cases where a complaint alleges that a school's action or policy excludes or discriminates against a person on the basis of sex, the Bostock opinion guides the Office of Civil Rights' understanding. That is, any discrimination against a person based on their sexual or gender identity generally involves discrimination on the basis of sex. Therefore, any school that receives federal funding from the U.S. Department of Education "has an obligation to protect all students, including LGBTQ students, from unlawful sex discrimination." We believe that this is a start in the right direction for more inclusive federal policies enacted and carried out in schools.

Even if the policy is designed to protect all students and encourage participation, the illusion of exclusion has led to severe consequences. Recently, the Trevor Project (2021) released a study showing that many LGBTQ youth still chose not to participate in sports due to discrimination or fear of discrimination based on their LGBTQ identities. One youth described, "I'm scared I will be harassed because of my sexuality." This research is devastating because sports could build unity, community, and important leadership skills. The Trevor Project (2021) reports that there are LGBTQ youth that play sports and do state that they receive these associated benefits, however, policies are needed that, "expand access to the positive benefits of sports rather than prohibiting youth from being able to access the positive aspects of sports."

Today, in the early 2020s, trans athletes are also fighting for their humanity as state after state attempts to pass legislation to ban transgender girls from participating in school sports. Such laws require trans youth to compete in sports according to their sex assigned at birth. These laws fail to recognize the importance of sports inclusion for transgender youth and ignore evidence that medical therapies equalize the playing field (Goldberg 2021).

FIGURE 5.7
Source: FOTOGRAFIA INC

Policies on Bathroom Usage

FIGURE 5.8
Source: JannHuizenga

Another important example of cis- and heteronormative policies in school settings is bathrooms. Public bathrooms are gendered institutions and the politics of bathrooms have increasingly become a topic of public debate. Gendered institutions affirm and enforce both gender and sex differences as inequality, including the intimate discussion of body mechanics. Bathrooms are sex segregated and, in this way, uphold the gender binary. Providing different bathrooms for males/boys/men and females/girls/women also assumes that everyone needs to protect their private parts from the "other" sex, but not from the same sex. This a good example of heteronormativity.

According to Wade and Ferree (2015, 2019), the idea that men and women should have separate bathrooms began during the 1800s. During this time in the United States, men and women were working in factories, and the idea of women working alongside men and sharing bathrooms challenged all ideas associated with Victorianism. Victorianism emphasized the belief that men and women are different and should be separate in almost all tasks. This thinking promoted *gender as difference* (West and Zimmerman 1987), with women being fragile and in need of separation from men. This separation also allowed women to continue to conceal their bodily functions, which allowed men to continue believing that women don't have the same bodily functions as men. In 1887, Massachusetts became one of the first states to put a law in place supporting sex-segregated bathrooms. By 1920, 43 other states followed Massachusetts, and provisions for separate bathrooms were put in place throughout the country (Stewart and Stewart 2020). This is a clear example of law shaping culture, emphasizing that gender and sex differences matter, and women and men, male and female, need differing public experiences.

Bathrooms Today and Current Policies

Everyone understands the importance of having access to bathrooms. Medical research has articulated many times that lack of access to public bathrooms is a health risk and can lead to infection (Davis 2015). As such, students who identify as nonbinary, genderqueer, trans, or nonconforming may have difficulty in using the "right bathroom." Eliminating sex-segregated bathrooms, or at a minimum requiring the provision of some gender-inclusive ones, are policies that would help trans and nonbinary people, but would also help cis people because more bathrooms for everyone is a good thing. The distribution of binary bathroom facilities is a testament to the knowledge that separate is not equal. We've all seen long lines outside of women's bathrooms, while the men's line is considerably shorter. While the goal is to reduce stress and increase the access to bathrooms for trans and nonbinary people, the binary approach to bathrooms can cause everyone problems.

FIGURE 5.9
Source: Infographic by Alex J. Mack

Nineteen states have passed laws protecting trans people's right to use the bathroom of their choice in any public place. On the other hand, from 2013 to 2016, at least 24 states considered "bathroom bills," or legislation that would restrict access to multiuser restrooms, locker rooms, and other sex-segregated facilities because of a definition of sex or gender consistent with sex assigned at birth or "biological sex" (Kralik 2019). North Carolina was the only state to enact this type of legislation. In North Carolina, the law stated that in government buildings, individuals (such as students at state-operated schools) may only use restrooms and changing facilities that correspond to the sex identified on their birth certificates.

Since sex is not visible, but gender is, how do we know each other's sex? Do people really need to carry around their birth certificate to show others before entering a bathroom? Thankfully, due to the efforts of trans people, in 2019, a federal court ruled this law could not stop trans and nonbinary people from using the bathroom that aligned with their gender identity.

Schools, an institution accessed by almost all people in the United States, are often left in a very tricky position as they need to follow the law to maintain funding and state support. Most schools, particularly public schools, are bound by state and federal law, which don't always support trans and nonbinary people. Many people, including lawmakers, confuse and conflate gender and sex (Mayers 2017). On the other hand, many educators want to accommodate the growing number of transgender students (Watkins and Mereno 2017). Educators who advocate for their trans students know that "transgender students want to be treated as the person they aspire to be rather than the one assigned at birth" (Ferfloia 2013).

Oftentimes, transgender students get lost in this debate and have articulated time and time again how the lack of access to safe bathrooms is emotionally and physically harmful (GLSEN 2020; Society for Adolescent Health and Medicine; Wernick, Kulick, and Chin 2017). As Watkins and Mereno (2017:169) report, "Sadly many schools have no specific policy in place, relying on state legislative language, which in many cases does not protect the rights of transgender students." With the legal complications associated with gender-inclusive bathrooms, we suggest signage that allows any student, regardless of sex or gender, access to any bathroom. As Wermick et al. (2017) articulate, feeling safe while using school facilities is necessary; safety and wellbeing are correlated with success, and the more students have access to bathrooms without ridicule or harassment, the better for *all* students.

Gendered Bullying

School and classroom policies against gender bullying must be clear, transparent, and carried out appropriately. The gender binary sets up a social hierarchy, and gender bullying is a tactic students use to move up this hierarchy. Students strictly police conventional gender norms, and gender-expansive behavior can result in harsh social punishment—ridicule, exclusion, even violence. Steele and Cohn-Vargas (2013) call for teachers to use real-life experiences to question hierarchical relationships,

FIGURE 5.10
Source: Marcos Calvo

and nowhere is this call more urgent than in gender politics at school. Research links gender-based bullying to low self-esteem, poor academic performance, elevated levels of depression, and increased risk of suicide during adolescence (Morrow 2004; Russell, Sinclair, Poteat, and Koenig 2012; Williams, Connolly, Pepler, and Craig 2005; Yunger, Carver, and Perry 2004). Gender-based victimization at school has long-term effects on psychological development that persist into adulthood (Toomey and Ryan 2010).

Research on bullying reveals a clear gender gap: cisgender heterosexual girls are harassed at a higher rate than cisgender heterosexual boys at every school level, with disparities increasing with age (Rich 2014). Forty-eight percent of girls report exposure to relational aggression, a phenomenon ascribed primarily to girls who manipulate and emotionally bully other girls (often covertly) to gain social status (Nishioka et al. 2011; Wiseman 2016).

Research also shows that conforming to traditional concepts of masculinity interferes with psychological development in boys and has detrimental effects on their mental and physical health. Because boys are so often socialized to externalize emotional distress, they are more likely to be diagnosed with learning difficulties and conduct disorders than mental disorders. Because boys are socialized to be self-reliant, they are also less likely to ask for help when they need it (APA, Boys and Men Guidelines Group 2018).

One area of bullying that is often overlooked or downplayed in schools is bullying of cisgender (and presumably heterosexual) boys. For instance, a cis boy calling another cis boy a sissy, gay, or a girl is problematic and must be met head on. Degrading other cis boys by calling them gay or feminine demeans everyone. Often young boys say that they would never use a slur like gay against someone whom they thought was gay; nevertheless, the mere fact that this can be used as a slur conveys the message that being gay is not as good as being straight (see Pascoe 2007). It also creates an environment where cis boys are not allowed to show appropriate emotions and be themselves for fear of being called a girl or feminine. This demeans girls and requires suppressing appropriate caring emotions.

Young men frequently describe the pressures they feel to define their masculinity in terms of cisgender and heterosexual identities. No matter what their sexual identity is or how many people they love who are gay, they, nonetheless, feel that they need to guard against being stereotyped as "gay." To protect themselves from homophobic slurs, they sometimes adopt a hypermasculine stance.

Daniel, an eighth-grade cis identifying boy, wrote about his gender experience: "I wish I could live in a world where I don't have to follow these rules to be accepted. I want to be able to express love for my family, loved ones, and friends without getting weird looks. Any show of affection for a male friend and it's 'Fag.' 'Gay.' 'Queer.' Any show of affection for a female friend and it's "Ooh, you *like* her. Are you guys going to start dating?'" He concluded with "All love is outlawed for my gender."

Educators must be prepared to deal with gender bullying in all its forms. If students see that you do not respond, they may take this as a sign that you support the bully, and unfortunately, this is exactly what most students see (Trevor Project 2020). When adults tolerate assaultive language and behaviors that target vulnerable students, it causes harm that manifests in the form of school absences, poor mental health, lower self-esteem, and higher rates of suicide.

Safe Zones and Gay/Straight Alliances

A Gay-Straight Alliance, Gender-Sexuality Alliance (GSA), or Queer-Straight Alliance (QSA) is a student-led or community-based organization, found in middle schools and high schools, as well as colleges and universities, primarily in the United States and Canada. The intention of these groups is to provide a safe and supportive environment for LGBTQ children, teenagers, and youth, as well as their cisgender heterosexual allies. In middle schools and high schools, GSAs are sponsored by a responsible teacher.

The first GSAs were established in the 1980s. In 1998, the first lawsuit defending students' right to form a GSA in a public school was filed. Since then, GSAs have prevailed in at least 17 federal EAA lawsuits, and the ACLU was involved in 14 of those cases. The U.S. Department of Education has also affirmed students' rights under the EAA, and GSAs now exist in every state in thousands of schools.

In addition to American Civil Liberties Union support, scientific studies show that GSAs have positive academic, health, and social impacts on school children of a minority sexuality or gender identity. A GLSEN (2020) research brief on GSA's makes the argument that the very presence of GSAs may help to make schools safer for LGBTQ students by sending a message that biased language and harassment will not be tolerated. In the same report, GSAs are stated to make school more accessible to LGBTQ students by contributing to a more positive school environment. Finally, the report argues that not enough schools have GSA's.

Safe Zones are another important training tool for educating students and teachers about LGBTQ issues and creating a safer environment for all students at school. For instance, The SafeZone

Initiative "trains educators, students, as well as LGBTQ folks on how to create a comfortable and welcoming space for students and peers." Overall, The SafeZone Initiative defines safe zones as

> Not just a place! It's also a frame of mind and a way to embody and carry yourself. A non-judgmental environment that promotes honest dialogues where folks can bring their authentic and holistic identities without fear of being discriminated against based on gender identity, gender expression, or orientation. The SafeZone Initiative was set in place to create more visibility for the LGBTQ community and allies, increase knowledge and provide skills to individuals or organizations to address the barriers in place for LGBTQ folks and help and empower people to advocate for equity across the board.
> (The SafeZone Initiative 2021 https://www.theszinitiative.org/)

Marni has been trained by this organization and has found their work very useful on her college campus. We know there are many wonderful organizations out there wanting to serve the LGBTQ community and educators specifically. Please do your due diligence when determining which organization is the right fit for your needs.

Gender and Sexuality Diversity Statements

In many parts of society, normalizing best and inclusive practices starts with writing down statements and policies. What is on paper can help redefine norms and school culture. Schools can support LGBTQ identifying students with an inclusivity policy that sends a clear message to the school community.

For example, The City Schools of Decatur (Decatur, Georgia) Board of Education issued an Equal Educational Opportunities policy in 2017 that said they were "committing to ensure that all students feel safe, supported, and valued." The board stated that the Equal Educational Opportunities policy (2017) includes protections related to gender identity. The board committed to participating in community events offering learning opportunities in this area and to gather input from the community on the policy. The goal remains to ensure that all students feel safe, supported, and valued; "We support our transgender students, staff, and community members and look forward to more clearly articulating that support in our policies."

In another example, the board of directors at Bridgestone Montessori School wrote a strongly worded policy followed by an email from the head of school announcing that children's gender and sexual identities would be accepted and respected by faculty, staff, students, and other parents. Students who changed their names or pronouns would have their choices honored. When Bridgestone had their first transgender student, they converted their bathrooms from "girl" and "boy" to single stall nongendered bathrooms throughout the school. That same year, when the elementary students took a camping trip, their trans boy student bunked with the other boys.

Similarly, we have seen schools strive for inclusion by changing the criteria for parents. For example, some schools have changed the name of events called "Donuts for Dads" and "Muffins for Moms" to "Pastries for Parents" to include LGBTQ couples. Or another easy change is to revise forms to read "Parent 1" and "Parent 2," instead of "Mother" and "Father."

These examples demonstrate ways that schools and associated districts can become more inclusive and welcoming to students regardless of family makeup. Lenora, the assistant principal at Bridgestone, emphasizes the need to have ongoing conversations about gender and sexuality, not only with students, but with parents too. Lenora said:

> With any subject regarding sexuality, there can be some embarrassment in discussing these issues with students. I have experienced parents hesitant to discuss these

issues, but I believe it's tied to their discomfort in discussing ANY aspect of sexuality as it relates to their children.

Bridgestone offers community forums for parents to discuss how they talk to their children about gender and sexuality. They share ideas, stories, and concerns. The school provides expert speakers, recommended reading, and book lists of inclusive story books for children.

Lenora works with the school diversity, equity, and inclusion task force to develop programs for students, faculty training, and parent education. According to Lenora:

> As a gay educator, I have always relied on my straight colleagues to help normalize LGBTQ issues because it doesn't always feel safe for me to be out. I was outed once as a teacher and had to discuss that with my students. It was a difficult conversation for me, and yet one of those former students is now a lesbian teacher, so I hope that conversation was of help to her.

Through our work consulting with school leaders, we have developed a set of practical steps to guide the process of writing a comprehensive gender and sexuality inclusion statement.

1. Make sure that the process of developing the statement is itself inclusive. So often, we see school leaders developing policies without the people who will be most impacted by the policy sitting at the table. Not only should your committee represent a diverse group of gender and sexual identities, but the people whose identities are most socially marginalized should be empowered to lead the process. Before any policy statement is published, it necessarily needs to be reviewed and approved by community members whose identities it most concerns.

2. Examine the vision, values, and mission of your school. What is your school's vision of a gender and sexually diverse and equitable community? How does gender and sexual inclusivity reflect your school's core values? How is inclusion a part of your mission? When a school's inclusion statement reflects the organization's vision, values, and mission, it carries more force in the community and is more likely to become a core part of the school's identity.
3. Review statements made by other schools. Many schools have diversity and inclusion statements posted on their websites and examining the scope of such statements can help guide the process of determining what you want your statement to convey. Some diversity and inclusion statements address gender and sexuality inclusion more specifically than others.
4. Center your "why." Communicating why a gender and sexuality inclusion policy or statement is important is central to your message. Why is the statement necessary? Who will be supported and protected by it? What issues will the statement include? Will it address bathrooms, chosen names, preferred pronouns, gender bullying, and/or safe zones? What expectations do you have for your community? The "why" of a gender and sexuality inclusion statement should include the interests and express the benefits to people of all identities yet center the needs of the people with the most marginalized identities.
5. Make the statement comprehensive but keep it as brief and succinct as possible. A statement that explains why the policy is important and necessary will pack power into fewer words. If the statement is too long and wordy, it will not engage your audience.
6. Provide supporting data. If you have research that confirms the need for your statement or policy, include citations or links to such data.

7. Craft a powerful headline. A headline is the simplest way to encompass the purpose and meaning of your statement.
8. Communicate widely and consistently. We cannot overemphasize the need for clear and consistent communication from school leaders concerning diversity and inclusion initiatives. Use multiple channels to communicate your commitment to gender and sexuality inclusion in your school. A communication plan might include posting your statement on the website, an email announcing it to parents, and a prominent position in the school newsletter.

Conclusion

Some schools have taken steps to remedy the negative impact of gendered conditioning. When Lenora's school had their first openly transgender student, they responded with a strongly worded inclusivity policy that sent a clear message to faculty, students, and parents. The policy stated that the school faculty would respect the name and pronoun choices of their students. They also converted their bathrooms from "girl" and "boy" to single stall, nongendered bathrooms throughout the school.

FIGURE 5.11
Source: Infographic by Alex J. Mack

Likewise, when Jack had a child in his class who identified as transgender, even though it was new to him and to the school, he responded by affirming the child's identity and expression. "We partnered with the parents, following their guidance to ensure that we were supporting the child in ways that felt comfortable for them," said Jack. "We teamed with the school administration in our efforts to help the child feel included, loved, and supported."

It is the school faculty's responsibility to protect the rights and safety of children in our care (Connell 2015). It is time for more schools to make clear policies and statements that support gender diversity and inclusion. As educators, we can "push back" against the institutions of gender and sexuality and reshape them to reduce the harm they cause.

Schools across the country are beginning to take steps to codify and institutionalize ideas of inclusivity by using statements and policies as well as being clear and transparent about the adaptability of historical policies, such as Title IX. We have seen schools support programs, student clubs/associations, and professional development for faculty and staff that builds on inclusive frameworks and offers development in these areas. We have also seen teachers take steps to create classroom policies that reflect practices of acceptance while standing up against discriminatory activities such as bullying. Oftentimes, without ideas written as policy they are not taken as seriously, and it can then be difficult to hold someone accountable to inclusive measures. Overall, we urge all educators to think seriously about their vision of an inclusive community and how they can make that vision a reality.

Conclusion

Looking Forward

Book Summary

We have covered a lot of ground in the previous five chapters with the intention of creating inclusive classroom communities for all students. In Chapter 1, we looked at the individual experiences of gender and sexuality, arguing that sex and gender are different categories and should be treated as such. We spent time breaking down all the situations that can impact individuals, including gender expression and identity, and as teachers how we can best honor and serve the diverse genders of our students.

In Chapter 2, we discussed how to disrupt unconscious bias and microaggressions. Here we looked at how to engage in self-reflective work. This can be challenging and uncomfortable, but we believe that it is necessary to uncover where and how we have bias and the impact it has on our interactions with students in the classroom. We also spent time talking about the importance of names, pronouns, and honorifics. We highlighted how to use chosen names and preferred pronouns. We wrapped up the chapter emphasizing that mistakes will happen, and that is why practicing and modeling this work is very important.

In Chapter 3, we focused on gender and sexuality experiences in the classroom. We addressed curriculum, both formal and hidden, and the way representations of diverse genders and sexualities matter to creating inclusive spaces. This is very important when it comes to confidence, achievement, and combating bullying. We also spent time in this chapter looking at the impact of race, poverty, and ability because gender and sexuality do not happen in isolation but at the intersection of other social categories. Finally, we looked at what it means for teachers to be out in the classroom. We understand that for many teachers, there is risk associated with being out; however, we discuss the benefits of being out, not just for one's self, but for students as well.

Chapter 4 covered the application of gender-aware pedagogy; here, we demonstrated how to affirm, validate, and empower students' gender and sexual identities. Gender-aware pedagogy is informed by other theories and strategies, particularly the work of Paulo Freire and bell hooks. We provided practical steps for a teacher to take to engage with this pedagogical practice and transform the classroom.

Chapter 5 looked at the institutional nature of schools, and how as an organization, schools have embeddet discriminatory practices that can and should be addressed. We spent time explaining how institutions, like schools, are gendered and the impact this has on students. We looked at policies, programs, and plans that support gender and sexual inclusivity in both the classroom and the larger school setting. We addressed existing policies and practices, such as sex education curriculum and Title IX, that have paved the way for some inclusion, but still have room for growth when it comes to trans, nonbinary, and intersex students. We spent time talking about bathrooms and how the necessary bodily practice of going to the bathroom has been gendered in a way that has led to various degrees of inequality. We also discussed how to create safe opportunities for students and staff, including but not limited to Safe Zones, Gay–Straight Alliances, and Diversity Statements.

Why This Work Matters

According to Gallup's latest survey in 2020, 5.6 percent of adults in the United States identify at LGBTQ (Jones 2021). This is up over one percentage point from the last time it was measured in 2017 (4.5 percent). The same poll shows that more than half (54.6 percent) of LGBTQ adults in the United States identify as bisexual, followed by 24.5 percent who indicate they are gay, 11.7 percent lesbian, and 11.3 percent as transgender (Jones 2021).

Jones (2021) explains, "One of the main reasons LGBT identification has been increasing over time is that younger generations are far more likely to consider themselves something other than heterosexual." In fact, while only 1.3 percent of Traditionalists (born before 1946), 2 percent of Baby Boomers (born 1946–1964), and 3.8 percent of Generation Z (born 1965–1980) consider themselves LBGTQ, this number jumps tremendously for Millennials (born 1981–1996) at 9.1 percent and Generation Z (born 1997–2002) at 15.9 percent (Jones 2021).

This means that at the time of the 2020 Gallup survey, one in six adult members of Generation Z identified as nonheterosexual. Furthermore, a new study from the Trevor Project shows that 26 percent of queer Generation Z people identify as gender nonbinary (Lopez 2021). Of those one in four queer youth who identify as nonbinary, less than six percent use exclusively he/him or she/her pronouns (Lopez 2021). Meaning the majority use they or some combination of pronouns.

As of the writing of this book, K-12 educators are currently working with Generation Z (born between approximately 1997 and 2012) and Generation Alpha (born between approximately 2012 and 2025) students. Generation Z is currently the queerest generation ever, and there are no signs indicating that this trend will reverse anytime soon. If 15.9 percent of Generation Z adults identify as LGBTQ, then we can assume that at least that percentage or higher of our students will at some point identify as nonheterosexual or noncisgender. This means that understanding gender and sexuality is more important than ever to our children.

These rapid changes in society also mean that things are changing at a faster pace than the research can keep up with. In many cases, educators and administrators in K-12 education are going to be on the front lines of this change. It also means that we are going to have to step back and let the kids take the lead. As Caldwell and Frame (second edition, 2022) argue in *Let's Get Real: Exploring Race, Class, and Gender Identities in the Classroom*:

> Our students deserve to have their complex identities and rich funds of knowledge recognized as their fundamental educational right.... As we have seen in classroom after classroom after classroom, when students feel valued, when they are given a voice, they rise to the occasion.

If we could provide one piece of advice to end this book, it would be to make sure that students feel valued and to let the kids take the lead. Believe students when they tell you that their gender and/or sexuality does not align with the binary categories we were taught. The younger generations have better vocabulary and language than we did to describe the nuances of gender and sexuality (Lopez 2021). Therefore, as adults, we can listen, learn, and support. Whether you like the way gender and sexuality is changing or not, the research is clear that we are moving in a direction of more openness and less rigidity. Educators must be willing to accept our students as they are, and more and more, that is going to be queer.

To be clear, we do not simply believe more and more youth are becoming queer, rather more and more youth can explore gender and sexuality in ways we did not before, and there is more acceptance in society for gender and sexual fluidity. This does not mean that queer students are being accepted across the board but through technology and especially social media, youth across the globe are able to find others like themselves and to put language to feelings in ways that were unavailable to many of us.

We hope that as an educator your number one goal is to meet the needs of students and to teach them. If this is your goal, then being open minded, willing to learn, and prepared to teach about gender and sexuality is a must. Whatever the outcome of this shift in society, it is up to us to lead the next generation and make sure that they are all safe and loved along the way.

Further Recommendations

To review the material, we have covered throughout the book, we recommend this brief summary of best practices for ways educators and schools can support their students on individual, interactional, and institutional levels.

- Honor students' pronoun choices and chosen names.
- List your pronouns on all identifying material—on name badges, email signature, with your screen name on virtual platforms, on social media accounts. This sends the message that you are aware and accepting of gender variations.
- Acknowledge safe spaces. Use rainbow colors or other signifiers to let students know they are welcome and accepted.
- Represent diverse gender and sexual identities via curriculum: reading materials, literature lessons, history lessons, posters, and classroom décor. Let students see reflections of themselves in your classroom and school.
- Support LGBTQ educators who choose to be out in their classrooms. Recognize that when teachers can be their authentic selves with their students, it empowers teaching and learning. Teaching is strongly impacted by relationships between teachers and students, and when teachers are required to exclude important aspects of their identities from students, it does not serve anyone.
- Offer safe spaces for students with diverse gender and sexual identities. Provide gay/straight alliances and affinity groups for students with diverse gender and sexual

identities. In such spaces, students who share common identity experiences find mutual support and encouragement in what otherwise may be a hostile environment.
- Offer gender and sexuality affinity groups for LGBTQ educators. These spaces provide institutional support for these educators by affirming their identities and establishing spaces where they can share common challenges, strengths, and resources for self-care.
- Offer ally groups as places for cisgender straight educators to learn from each other how to best supports students and colleagues with gender and sexuality marginalized identities, so that the burden of educating others doesn't fall solely on the shoulders of those most impacted by discrimination.
- Develop a strongly worded inclusivity policy that makes the message clear: Students will be supported in their gender and sexuality development, bathrooms are non-gendered, pronoun choices and chosen names of students will be honored.
- Send a clear and consistent message that cascades down from top leadership to every level of the school, including board, administrators, faculty and staff, support personnel, students, parents, and vendors.
- Deliver regular training on gender and sexuality education best practices.

While this list is not conclusive or exhaustive, these practices include important steps that can move us toward a vision of more gender and sexually diverse, just, equitable, and inclusive school communities.

Glossary of Key Terms

The terms and definitions below are always evolving and changing and often mean different things to different people. They are provided as a starting point for discussion and understanding.

Agender—An individual who does not identify with any gender and/or rejects the idea of gender for themselves.

Androgynous—A gender presentation that combines stereotypical masculine and feminine gender expressions.

Aromatic—A romantic orientation often characterized by not feeling romantic attraction or a desire for romance. Aromantic people can be satisfied by friendship and other non-romantic relationships. Aromantic individuals can also identify with another sexual identity.

Asexual—A broad spectrum of sexual orientations generally characterized by feeling varying degrees of sexual attraction or a desire for partnered sexuality. An asexual person might not experience sexual attraction but can experience other forms of attraction such as romantic and or emotional attraction.

Bi+—A person whose sexual attraction and affectional orientation to more than one gender/sex, or regardless of gender/sex; including, but not limited to, pansexual, bisexual, queer, etc.; an umbrella term for anyone who does not identify as monosexual.

Biphobia—Systematic oppression of people who are sexually or romantically attracted to both, or multiple, sexes and genders.

Cisgender/Cis—A person whose gender identity or performance in a gender role aligns with the sex they were assigned at birth. The prefix cis- means "on this side of" or "not across." Cis a term used to highlight the privilege of people that are not transgender.

Cisnormativity—An assumption that everyone's gender identity matches the sex they were assigned at birth.

Cissexism—Discrimination against and the oppression of trans and gender nonbinary people based on the idea that cisgender identities are "natural" or "correct" compared to trans identities.

Compulsory heterosexuality—A feeling of obligation to heterosexuality that is a byproduct of heteronormativity, or the assumption that heterosexuality and being cisgender is the social norm.

Demisexual—Demisexuality is when someone feels sexual attraction only to people with whom they have an emotional bond. Most demisexuals feel sexual attraction rarely compared to the general population, and some have little to no interest in sexual activity.

Drag King—Any person (regardless of sex or gender identity) who performs masculinity within the context of a drag show or performance.

Drag Queen—Any person (regardless of sex or gender identity) who performs femininity within the context of a drag show or performance.

Femme—Historically used in the lesbian community, it is being increasingly used by other LGBTQIA people to describe gender expressions that reclaim and disrupt traditional constructs of femininity.

Gay—A sexual orientation toward people of the same gender; used as an umbrella term for any individual who is attracted to members of their same gender.

Gender—A set of cultural, behavioral, and physical expectations placed on people, usually based on their assumed sex; a socially constructed spectrum of masculinity and femininity; includes identity and expression.

Gender Binary—The idea that there are only two gender categories that people fit into: men and women.

Gender Confirmation Surgeries or Gender Affirmation Surgeries—Refers to a number of surgical procedures that some trans people have in order to better align their biological sex and body with the expectations of the gender they identify with; these procedures include, but are not limited to: top surgery (having breast removed, enlarged, or reduced), bottom surgery (reconstruction on a person's genitals to align them more closely with their gender identity); and facial reconstruction procedures. These procedures were previously referred to as sex reassignment surgeries (SRS).

Gender Expansive—An umbrella term used for individuals who broaden their own culture's commonly held definitions of gender, including expectations for its expression, identities, roles, and/or other perceived gender norms. Gender expansive individuals include those who identify as transgender, as well as anyone else whose gender in some way is seen to be broadening the surrounding society's notion of gender.

Gender Expression—How one expresses oneself in terms of dress and behavior. The parts of gender that are externally and socially performed to be seen by others; can include a person's behaviors, dress, mannerisms, speech patterns, and social interactions. Sometimes known as Gender Presentation.

Gender Fluid—A person whose gender identification and expression shifts. Being fluid in motion between two or more genders.

Gender Identity—An individual's sense of themselves as a man, a woman, trans, etc. How an individual recognizes their own gender, or lack thereof, and exists in the world as a result.

Gender nonconforming—Adjective for people who do not subscribe to societal expectations of typical gender expressions or roles. The term is more commonly used to refer to gender expression (how one behaves, acts, and presents themselves to others) as opposed to gender identity (one's internal sense of self).

Gender Queer—A gender identity and/or expression that falls outside of societal norms. To be beyond genders or is some combination of them.

Heteronormativity—Attitudes, behaviors, and a belief system that assumes the gender binary, ignoring genders besides women and men, and that people should and will align with conventional expectations of society for gender identity, gender expression, and sexual and romantic attraction. The assumption that everyone is heterosexual.

Heterosexism—The assumption that all people are or should be heterosexual. Heterosexism excludes the needs, concerns, and life experiences of lesbian, gay, bisexual, and queer people while it gives advantages to heterosexual people. Discrimination against and oppression of sexual minorities, including gay, lesbian, bi, asexual, etc.

Heterosexual/Straight—A sexual orientation in which a person who is sexually and/or romantically attracted to the opposite sex or gender.

Homonormativity—The normalization of heterosexuality into culture, which results in a hierarchy among sexual minorities where more value is placed on those who conform to heterosexist institutions and norms, such as getting married and raising children.

Homophobia—Systemic oppression of people who are sexually or romantically attracted to the same sex or gender.

Homosexual/Homosexuality—An outdated term used to describe a person who is sexually or romantically attracted to people of the same sex or gender; historically, this term was widely used, but is generally not preferred by the queer community anymore because of the term's connection with mental illness and pathologization.

Hormone Replacement Therapy (HRT)—The process of changing one's body's hormones in order to change physical features to better align with the expectations of one's gender identity; for trans men this usually means taking testosterone and for trans women taking estrogen; importantly, not all trans people choose to take hormones.

Intersectionality—A term coined by law professor Kimberlé Crenshaw in the 1980s to describe the way that multiple systems of oppression interact in the lives of those with multiple marginalized identities. The numerous and varied ways individuals' identities (e.g., gender, race, sexuality, social class, ability) interact and interlock to shape their experience of the world, resulting in various degrees of privilege and oppression.

Intersex—An umbrella term for individuals who were born with a wide range of sex characteristics that do not align with conventional understandings of the binary "female" or "male."

Lesbian—Usually refers to women, as well as other individuals who are aligned with womanhood, whose primary sexual and affectional orientation is toward people of the same gender; women or feminine people.

LGBTQ+—An abbreviation to refer to lesbian women, gay men, bisexual people, trans people, and queer people; sometimes the Q is also used for questioning; the plus sign at the end signifies that this is not an inclusive list; for example, often the acronym also includes an I for intersex and an A for asexual.

Monosexuality—Sexual and/or romantic attraction to members of one sex or gender category, includes, but not limited to, gay, lesbian, and heterosexual.

Nonbinary—An individual who identifies outside of the gender binary of man and woman. A gender identity and experience that embraces a full universe of expressions. For some, it could be an active resistance to the binary. For some people who identify as nonbinary, there may be overlap with other concepts and identities like gender expansive and gender non-conforming.

Pansexual, (Omnisexual)—Terms used to describe people who have romantic, sexual, or affectional desire for people of all genders and sexes. Has some overlap with bisexuality.

Passing—Being seen or read by others as the gender one identifies with, rather than the sex they were categorized as at birth.

Queer—Inclusive term for individuals and a community who identify with non-normative genders and sexualities; including but not limited to lesbian, gay, bisexual, transgender, asexual, pansexual, genderqueer, nonbinary, etc.. This term has historically been used in derogatory ways, but many people have reclaimed it as an expression of power and freedom.

Questioning—The process of exploring one's own gender identity, gender expression, and/or sexual orientation. Some people may also use this term to name their identity within the LGBTQIA community.

Sex—The biological characteristics (genitalia, chromosomes, and hormones) used to divide humans into categories of male and female; also includes intersexuality.

Sexism—The cultural, institutional, and individual set of beliefs and practices that privilege men, subordinate women, and devalue ways of being that are associated with women.

Sexual assault—Unwanted sexual contact, including but not limited to touching and fondling; sometimes used synonymously with rape.

Sexual harassment—Unwelcome sexual advances, requests for sexual favors, or other verbal or physical harassment of a sexual nature.

Sexuality—Identities based on a person's sexual and romantic attractions, or lack thereof.

Social Institution—An interrelated system of social roles and social norms, organized around the satisfaction of an important social need or social function. Social Institutions are organized patterns of beliefs and behavior that are centered on basic social needs.

Stereotyping—Assuming or generalizing about a person's characteristics or personality based on their association with specific groups, without regard for their individual differences.

Trans men—The variety of identities of individuals who were assigned female at birth based on interpretation of biology (sex), but who now identify their sex as male, their gender as man, or their gender expression as masculine.

Trans women—The variety of identities of individuals who were assigned male at birth based on interpretation of biology (sex), but who now identify their sex as female, their gender as woman, or their gender expression as feminine.

Transgender/trans—A person whose gender identity does not align with the sex they were assigned at birth; can be an identity or an umbrella category. The term trans acts as a more inclusive term than transgender for gender non-conforming and non-binary folks.

Transitioning—A catchall term used to describe the process of changing one's gender/sex to align more with one's identity;

this can include, but is not limited to, hormone replacement therapies, gender affirmation surgeries, and other social transitions, such as changing one's name or pronouns.

Transnormativity—The pressure for trans people to fit a cisgender presentation of what it means to be a man or women; creates a hierarchy of transness based on appearance and physical transitions.

Transphobia—Systematic oppression of people who do not identify with the gender that aligns with the sex they were assigned at birth.

Womxn—Some womxn spell the word with an "x" as a form of empowerment to move away from the "men" in the "traditional" spelling of women.

Note: These definitions were written for this project. They combine a number of resources and more information about them can be found by referring to the terms where they appear in the book. Importantly, definitions and concepts are continuously changing and vary based on time and social location. Therefore, these definitions are for the purposes of understanding this work in the current context and time.

Recommended Resources for Educators

Documentaries

Gender

American Transgender. National Geographic. 1999.

Bailey, F., & LaPiere, G., *Becoming Chaz*. World of Wonder Productions. 2011.

Chasnoff, D., *Straightlaced: How Gender's Got Us All Tied up*. New Day Films. 2009.

Chermayeff, M., *Half the Sky: Turning Oppression into Opportunity for Women Worldwide*. Roco Films. 2012.

Couric, K., *Gender Revolution: A Journey with Katie Couric*. 20th Century Fox Home Entertainment. 2017.

Davis, K., *Southern Comfort*. Q-Ball Productions, Inc. 2001.

Earp, J., *The Purity Myth: The Virginity Movement's War against Women*. Media Education Foundation. 2011.

Epstein, A., & Lake, R., *The Business of Being Born*. New Line Home Entertainment. 2008.

Goodman, B., *Makers: Women Who Make America*. PBS Distribution. 2013.

Goldberger, J., *Trans*. Wellspring Media. 2006.

Jorgensen, C., *Christine Jorgensen: A Personal Autobiography*. Cleis Press. 2000.

Katz, J., *Tough Guise 2: Violence, Manhood & American Culture*. Media Education Foundation. 2013.

Keith, T., *The Bro Code: How Contemporary Culture Creates Sexist Men*. Media Education Foundation. 2011.

Lambert, M., *14 Women*. Screen Media. 2007.

Muska, S., & Greta Olafsdottir, G., *The Brandon Teena Story*. New Video. 1999.

Newsom, J. S., *Miss Representation*. Roco Films Educational. 2011.

Newsom, J. S., *The Mask You Live in*. The Representation Project. 2015.

Pierson, F., *Soldier's Girl*. Showtime Entertainment. 2004.

Roberts, D., *America the Beautiful*. Xenon. 2007.

West, B., & Cohen, J., *My Name Is Pauli Murray*. Amazon Studios. 2021.

Sexuality

Davis, K., & Heilbroner, D., *Stonewall Uprising*. PBS Distribution. 2011.

Dick, K., *Outrage*. Magnolia Home Entertainment. 2009.

Dick, K., *The Invisible War*. Cinedigm Entertainment Group. 2012.

Dick, K., *The Hunting Ground*. RADiUS-TWC. 2015.

Gray, C., *I Can't Marry You*. FYI Productions. 2004.

Houston, J., *Let's Talk about Sex*. New Video Group. 2011.

Ingram, M., *Small Town Gay Bar*. Red Envelope Entertainment. 2007.

Josue, M., *Matt Shephard Is a Friend of Mine*. Logo Documentary Films. 2013.

Karslake, D. G., *For the Bible Tells Me So*. First Run Features. 2007.

Kates, N., & Singer, B., *Brother Outsider: The Life of Bayard Rustin*. Bayard Rustin Film Project. 2008.

Lipschutz, M., & Rosenblatt, R., *The Education of Shelby Knox: Sex, Lies & Education*. Docudrama. 2006.

Richen, Y., *The New Black: LGBT Rights and African American Communities*. California Newsreel. 2013.

Movies

Gender

Anderson, J., Coolidge, M, & Heche, A., *If These Walls Could Talk 2*. HBO Video. 2000.

Elliot, S., *Adventures of Priscilla, Queen of the Desert*. PolyGram Video. 1997.

Hooper, T., *The Danish Girl*. Focus Features. 2015.
Kidron, B., *Too Wong Foo, Thanks for Everything! Julie Newmar*. Amblin Entertainment, Universal. 1995.
Peirce, K., *Boys Don't Cry*. Twentieth Century Fox Home Entertainment. 2000.
Sciamma, C., *Tomboy*. Dada Films. 2011.
Tucker, D., *Transamerica*. IFC Films. 2006.

Sexuality

Cholodenko, L., *The Kids Are All Right*. Universal Studios Home Entertainment. 2010.
Demme, J., *Philadelphia*. Columbia TriStar. 1997.
Mulcahy, R., *Prayers for Bobby*. Once Upon a Times Films. 2009.
Rees, D., *Pariah*. Alliance/Universal. 2012.
Van Sant, G., *Milk*. Universal Pictures. 2009.

Academic/Non-Fiction

Gender

Adichie, C. N., *We Should All Be Feminists*. Anchor Books. 2015.
Beemyn, G. (Ed.), *Trans People in Higher Education*. State University of New York Press. 2019.
Brubaker, R., *Trans: Gender and Race in the Age of Unsettled Identities*. Princeton University Press. 2016.
Erickson-Schroth, L. (Ed.)., *Trans Bodies, Trans Selves*. Oxford University Press. 2014.
Gay, R., *Bad Feminist: Essays*. Harper Perennial. 2014.
Halberstam, J., *Trans*: A Quick and Quirky Account of Gender Variability*. University of California Press. 2018.
hooks, b., *Feminism Is for Everybody*. South End Press. 2000.
Lorde, A., *Sister Outsider: Essays and Speeches*. Crossing Press. 1984.
Meadow, T., *Trans Kids: Being Gendered in the Twenty-First Century*. University of California Press. 2018.

Pascoe, C. J., *Dude, You're a Fag: Masculinity and Sexuality in High School*. University of California Press. 2007.

Singh, A., *The Queer and Transgender Resilience Workbook: Skills for Navigating Sexual Orientation and Gender Expression*. New Harbinger Publications. 2018.

Stein, A., *Unbound: Transgender Men and the Remaking of Identity*. Vintage Books. 2019.

Taylor, J. K., Lewis, D. C., & Haider-Markel, D. P., *The Remarkable Rise of Transgender Rights*. University of Michigan Press. 2018.

Teich, N. M., *Transgender 101: A Simple Guide to a Complex Issue*. Columbia University Press. 2012.

Travers, A., *The Trans Generation: How Trans Kids (and Their Parents) Are Creating a Gender Revolution*. New York University Press. 2018.

Valenti, J., *The Purity Myth: How America's Obsession with Virginity Is Hurting Young Women*. Seal Press. 2010.

Valenti, J., *Full Frontal Feminism: A Young Woman's Guide to Why Feminism Matters*. Seal Press. 2014.

Sexuality

Barton, B., *Pray the Gay Away: The Extraordinary Lives of Bible Belt Gays*. New York University Press. 2012.

Canaday, M., *The Straight State: Sexuality and Citizenship in Twentieth-Century America*. Princeton University Press. 2009.

Erzen, T., *Straight to Jesus: Sexual and Christian Conversions in the Ex-Gay Movement*. University of California Press. 2006.

Howard, J., *Men Like That: A Southern Queer History*. University of Chicago Press. 2001.

Johnson, E. P., *Sweet Tea: Black Gay Men of the South*. University of North Carolina Press. 2008.

Orenstein, P., *Boys & Men: Young Men on Hookups, Love, Porn, Consent and Navigating the New Masculinity*. HarperCollins Publishers. 2020.

Biography

Chase, N. J., *Tea and Transition*. Telemachus Press. 2015.
Jennings, J., *Being Jazz: My Life as a (Transgender) Teen*. Crown. 2016.
Nutt, A. E., *Becoming Nicole: The Transformation of an American Family*. Random House. 2015.
Tobia, J., *Sissy: A Coming of Gender Story*. G. P. Putnam's Sons. 2019.

Books for Children

Bone, J., & Bone, L., *Not Every Princess*. Magination Press. 2014.
de Haan, L., *King and King*. Tricycle Press. 2005.
Gino, A., *George*. Scholastic, Inc. 2015.
Hall, M., *Red: A Crayon's Story*. Greenwillow Books. 2015.
Love, J., *Julian Is a Mermaid*. Candlewick Press. 2018.
Newman, L., *Daddy, Pappa, and Me*. Tricycle Press. 2008.
Newman, L., *Mommy, Mama, and Me*. Tricycle Press. 2008.
Newman, L., *Heather Has Two Mommies*. Candlewick Press. 2015.
Parr, T., *The Family Book*. Little, Brown and Company. 2010.
Pearlman, R., *Pink Is for Boys*. Running Press Kids. 2018.
Richardson, J., & Parnell, P., *And Tango Makes Three*. Little Simon. 2015.
Sima, J., *Not Quite Narwhal*. Simon & Schuster Books for Young Readers. 2017.
Smith, L. *Madam President*. Little, Brown Books for Young Readers. 2008.

Books for Teens/Young Adults

Albertalli, B., *Simon vs. the Homo Sapiens Agenda*. Balzer + Bray. 2015.
Chevat, R., & Bronski M. (2019). *A Queer History of the United States for Young People*. Beacon Press.

Gephart, D., *Lily and Duncan*. Penguin Random House. 2018.
Jordan, H., *When She Woke*. Algonquin Press. 2012.
Lo, M., *Last Night at the Telegraph Club*. Dutton Books. 2021.
Mitchell, S., *All Out: The No-Longer-Secret Stories of Queer Teens throughout the Ages*. Harlequin Teens. 2018.
Moulite, M., & Moutlite, M., *One of the Good Ones*. Inkyard Press/Harlequin Teen. 2022.
Petrus, J., *Stars and the Blackness between Them*. Dutton Books. 2019.
Polonsky, A., *Gracefully Grayson*. Hyperion. 2016.
Ruby, L., *Thirteen Doorways, Wolves behind Them All*. Balzer + Bray. 2019.
Saenz, B. A., *Aristotle and Dante Discover the Secrets of the Universe*. Simon & Schuster Books for Young Readers. 2014.
Shetterly, M. L., *Hidden Figures: The Untold Story of the African American Women Who Helped Win the Space Race*. HarperCollins Publishers. 2016.
Thomas, A., *Cemetery Boys*. Swoon Reads. 2020.
Wang, J., *The Princess and the Dressmaker*. First Second Books. 2018.
Watson, R., & Hagan, E., *Watch Us Rise*. Bloomsbury Publishing. 2019.
Woodson, J., *Harbor Me*. Penguin Random House. 2018.

Books for Older Teens/Adults

Adiche, C. N., *Purple Hibiscus*. Algonquin Books. 2012.
Atwood, M., *The Handmaid's Tale*. Anchor Books. 1985.
Baldwin, J., *Giovanni's Room*. Dial Press. 1956.
Brown, R. M., *Rubyfruit Jungle*. Bantam Books. 1988.
Chevat, R., & Bronski M. (2019). A Queer History of the United States for Young People. Beacon Press.
Eugenides, J., *Middlesex*. Picador/Farrar, Straus, Giroux. 2003.
Hawthorne, N., *The Scarlet Letter*. Holt, Rinehart and Winston. 1850.

Hurston, Z. N., *Their Eyes Were Watching God*. Harper Perennial Modern Classics. 1937.
Morrison, T., *Sula*. Vintage. 1973.
Naylor, G., *The Women of Brewster Place*. Penguin Books. 1983.
Piercy, M., *Woman on the Edge of Time*. Fawcett Crest. 1983.
Russ, J., *The Female Man*. Gregg Press. 1977.
Vuong, O., *On Earth We're Briefly Gorgeous*. Penguin Books. 2019.
Walker, A., *The Color Purple*. Mariner Books. 1982.

Workbooks

Bornstein, K., *My New Gender Workbook: A Step-by-Step Guide to Achieving World Peace through Gender Anarchy and Sex Positivity*. 2nd edition. 2013.
Singh, A., *The Queer and Transgender Resilience Workbook: Skills for Navigating Sexual Orientation and Gender Expression*. 2018.
Triska, A. M., *Gender Identity Workbook for Teens: Practical Exercises to Navigate YourExploration, Support Your Journey, and Celebrate Who You Are*. 2021.

Conferences/Workshops

Creating Change Conference. National LGBTQ Task Force.
The National LGBTQ Health Conference. Institute for Sexual and Gender Minority Health and Well Being. Northwestern University.
Southern Comfort Transgender Conference.

Organizations with Resources

ACLU—https://www.aclu.org
Bisexual Resource Center—https://www.biresource.org
Campaign for Southern Equality—https://www.southernequality.org

Gay, Lesbian, & Straight Education Network (GLSEN)—https://www.glsen.org
Gender Spectrum—https://www.genderspectrum.org
GLAAD—https://www.glaad.org
GSA Network—https://www.gsanetwork.org
Human Rights Campaign (HRC)—https://www.hrc.org
iChange Collaborative—https://www.ichangecollaborative.com
Matthew Shepard Foundation—https://www.matthewshepard.org
Movement Advancement Project (MAP)—https://www.lgbtmap.org
National Center for Lesbian Rights (NCLR)—https://www.nclrights.org
National Center for Transgender Equality—https://www.transequality.org
National LGBTQ Task Force—https://www.thetaskforce.org
National Resource Center on LGBT Aging—https://www.lgbtagingcenter.org
Parents, Families, and Friends of Lesbians and Gays (PFLAG)—https://www.pflag.org
Point Foundation—https://www.pointfoundation.org
Pronouns Matter: Resources on Personal Pronouns—https://www.mypronouns.org
Safe Schools Coalition—https://www.safeschoolscoalition.org
Scarleteen: Sex Ed for the Real World —https://www.scarleteen.com
Sylvia Rivera Law Project—https://www.srlp.org
The Trevor Project—https://www.thetrevorproject.org
The Williams Institute—https://www.williamsinstitute.law.ucla.edu

Transgender Law Center—https://www.transgender-lawcenter.org

Victory Fund—https://www.victoryfund.org

Pedagogy

Barnett, B., & Felton, P., *Intersectionality in Action: A Guide for Faculty and Campus Leaders for Creating Inclusive Classrooms and Institutions*. Stylus Publishing. 2016.

Caldwell, M., & Frame, O., *Let's Get Real: Exploring Race, Class, and Gender Identities in the Classroom*. Routledge. 2022.

Freire, P., *Pedagogy of the Oppressed*. The Seabury Press. 1970.

Freire, P., *Education for Critical Consciousness*. Seabury Press. 1973.

hooks, b., *Teaching to Transgress: Education as the Practice of Freedom*. Routledge. 1994.

hooks, b., *Teaching Critical Thinking: Practical Wisdom*. Routledge. 2010.

Samuels, D. R., *The Culturally Inclusive Educator: Preparing for a Multicultural World*. Teachers College Press. 2017.

Study Guide

Use the following questions to get more out of the book by discussing it with colleagues during team planning meetings, book studies, or schoolwide professional development sessions.

Chapter 1

1. How would you explain or describe the differences between sex, gender, and sexuality to your students? Why might it be important to make note of these differences?
2. What is gender expression and gender identity development? How do you see this expressed in your cis and trans/nonbinary students?

Chapter 2

1. How were you socialized regarding gender norms? How did your conditioning influence you as a learner?
2. What do you know now about gender and sexuality that you wish you had known when you were in school?
3. What would you like students to call you? Why do names matter?

Chapter 3

1. What has been your process in selecting a curriculum? What degree of autonomy do you have? What criteria do you want your curriculum to meet?
2. Does your school offer programs, clubs, activities, and/or events for students from diverse gender and sexuality identities? How are these programs perceived? Is there any stigma attached to them? How do these programs benefit LGBTQ students?

Chapter 4

1. Review the works of Paulo Freire (Pedagogy of the Oppressed, 1968) and bell hooks (Teaching to Transgress, 1994). How do these pedagogical masterpieces influence your pedagogy?
2. What is your teaching philosophy? Does it include a critically aware pedagogy?
3. How did you arrive at your pedagogical style? What teachers or theorists influenced you?

Chapter 5

1. Institutions are powerful organizations in our lives. How do you see education connected to other social institutions such as family, peer groups, sports, and the government?
2. How have you seen Title IX play out at your school?
3. Are bathrooms available with ease and comfort to all students? If not, what would it take to make this necessary bodily function a simple activity for students at your school? What concerns do folks have about bathrooms? How can you address these concerns?
4. In terms of gender and sexuality, what is your vision of an inclusive community?

References

Adichie, Chimamanda Ngozi. 2012. *Purple Hibiscus: A Novel*. Chapel Hill, NC: Algonquin Books.

Allison, Rachel. 2018. *Kicking Center: Gender and the Selling of Women's Professional Soccer*. New Brunswick, NJ: Rutgers University Press.

American Psychological Association. 2018. *APA Guidelines for Psychological Practice with Boys and Men*. https://www.apa.org/about/policy/boys-men-practice-guidelines.pdf

Apple, Michael W. 2019. "On Doing Critical Policy Analysis." *Educational Policy* 33(1):276–287.

Aulette, Judy Root, Judith Wittner, and Kristen Barber. 2015. *Gendered Worlds*. 4th edition. New York, NY: Oxford University Press.

Ball, Stephen J. 2010. "New Class Inequalities in Education: Why Education Policy May Be Looking in the Wrong Place! Education Policy, Civil Society and Social Class". *International Journal of Sociology and Social Policy* 30(3/4): 155–166.

Baxter-Magolda, Marcia B. 1999. *Creating Contexts for Learning and Self-authorship: Constructive-developmental Pedagogy*. Nashville, TN: Vanderbilt University Press.

Berger, Peter L., and Thomas Luckmann. 1966. *The Social Construction of Reality: A Treatise in the Sociology of Knowledge*. Garden City, NY: Doubleday.

Bertrand, Marianne, and Sendhil Mullainathan. 2004. "Are Emily and Greg More Employable Than Lakisha and Jamal? A Field Experiment on Labor Market Discrimination." *The American Economic Review* 9(4):991–1013.

Beauchamp, Catherine, and Lynn Thomas. 2009. "Understanding Teacher Identity: An Overview of Issues in the Literature and Implications for Teacher Education." *Cambridge Journal of Education* 39(20):175–189.

Blakemore, Judith E. Owen, Sheri A. Berenbaum, and Lynn S. Liben. 2012. *Gender Development*. New York, NY: Psychology Press.

Brey, Cristobal de Brey, Lauren Musu, Joel McFarland, Sidney Wilkinson-Flicker, Melissa Diliberti, Anlan Zhang, Claire Branstetter, and Xiaolei Wang. 2019. *Status and Trends in the Education of Racial and Ethnic Groups 2018*. National Center for Education Statistics. https://nces.ed.gov/pubs2019/2019038.pdf.

Bridges, Tristan. 2019. "The Costs of Exclusionary Practices in Masculinities Studies." *Men and Masculinities* 22(1):16–33.

Bridges, Tristan, and C. J. Pascoe. 2014. "Hybrid Masculinities: New Directions in the Sociology of Men and Masculinities." *Sociology Compass* 8(3):246–225.

Bronfenbrenner, Urie. 1979. *The Ecology of Human Development Experiments by Nature and Design*. Cambridge, MA: Harvard University Press.

Brown, Marni, and Mahala Dyer Stewart. 2018. *Frameworks of Inequality: Intersectional Perspective*. San Diego, CA: Cognella Academic Publishing.

Caldwell, Martha, and Oman Frame. 2022. *Let's Get Real: Exploring Race, Class, and Gender Identities in the Classroom*. 2nd edition. New York, NY: Routledge.

Carnevale, Anthony P., Megan L. Fasules, Michael C. Quinn, and Kathryn Peltier Campbell. 2019. *Born to Win, Schooled to Lose: Why Equally Talented Students Don't Get Equal Chances to Be All They Can Be*. https://files.eric.ed.gov/fulltext/ED599950.pdf

Carter, Prudence L. 2005. *Keepin it Real: School Success Beyond Black and White*. New York, NY: Oxford University Press.

Chick, Nancy, and Holly Hassel. 2009. "'Don't Hate Me Because I'm Virtual': Feminist Pedagogy in the Online Classroom." *Feminist Teacher* 19(3):195–215.

Child Trends 2019. https://www.childtrends.org/

Children's Defense Fund. 2021. The State of America's Children. https://www.childrensdefense.org/state-of-americas-children/

Chou, Rosalind S. 2012. *Asian American Sexual Politics: The Construction of Race, Gender, and Sexuality*. Lanham, MD: Rowman & Littlefield.

Chou, Rosalind S., and Joe R. Feagin. 2014. *The Myth of the Model Minority: Asian Americans Facing Racism*. 2nd edition. Boulder, CO: Routledge Press.

Chou, R., K. Lee, and S. Ho. 2015a. "Love Is (Color) Blind: Asian Americans and White Institutional Space at the Elite University." *Sociology of Race and Ethnicity* 1(2):302–316.

Chou, R., K. Lee, and S. Ho. 2015b. *Asian Americans on Campus: Racialized Space and White Power.* Routledge.

Clifford, Pat, and Susan J. Marinucci. 2008. "Voices Inside Schools: Testing the Waters: Three Elements of Classroom Inquiry." *Harvard Educational Review* 78(4):675–688.

Coleman, E. 1982. "Developmental Stages of the Coming-Out Process." *American Behavioral Scientist* 25(4):469–482.

Collins, Patricia Hill, and Sirma Bilge. 2016. *Intersectionality.* Cambridge: Polity Press.

Collins, Patricia Hill. 1990. *Black Feminist Thought: Knowledge, Consciousness, and the Politics of Empowerment.* London: HarperCollins.

Connell, Catherine. 2015. *School's Out: Gay and Lesbian Teachers in the Classroom.* 1st edition. Oakland: University of California Press.

Cooley, Charles Horton. 1902. *Human Nature and the Social Order.* New York, NY: Schocken.

Copur-Gencturk, Yasemin, Joseph R. Cimpian, Sarah Theule Lubienski, and Ian Thacker. 2020. "Teachers' Bias against the Mathematical Ability of Female, Black, and Hispanic Students." *Educational Researcher* 49(1):30–43.

Côté, James E., and Charles G. Levine. 2002. *Identity Formation, Agency, and Culture: A Social Psychological Synthesis.* Malwah, NJ: Lawrence Erlbaum Associates Publishers.

Coury, S., J. Huang, A. Kumar, S. Prince, A. Krivkovich, and L. Yee. 2020. "Women in the Workplace 2020." Joint report by Leanin.org and McKinsey. https://www.mckinsey.com/featured-insights/diversity-and-inclusion/women-in-the-workplace

Craig, Shelley L., and Mark S. Smith. 2014. "The Impact of Perceived Discrimination and Social Support on the School Performance of Multiethnic Sexual Minority Youth." *Youth & Society* 46(1):30–50.

Crenshaw, Kimberle. 1989. "Demarginalizing the Intersection of Race and Sex: A Black Feminist Critique of Antidiscrimination

Doctrine, Feminist Theory and Antiracist Politics." *University of Chicago Legal Forum* 1(8):139–167.

Crenshaw, Kimberle. 2016. *Ted Talk: The Urgency of Intersectionality*. https://www.ted.com/talks/kimberle_crenshaw_the_urgency_of_intersectionality/up-next?language=en

Cunha, Flavio, and James J. Heckman. 2009. "The Economics and Psychology of Inequality and Human Development." *Journal of the European Economic Association* 7(2–3):320–364.

D'Augelli, Anthony R., Neil W. Pilkington, and Scott L. Hershberger. 2002. "Incidence and Mental Health Impact of Sexual Orientation Victimization of Lesbian, Gay, and Bisexual Youths in High School." *School Psychology Quarterly* 17(2):148–167.

Davis, Georgiann. 2015. *Contesting Intersex: The Dubious Diagnosis*. New York, NY: New York University Press.

Dellenty, Shaun. 2019. *Celebrating Difference: A Whole School Approach to LGBT+ Inclusion*. London: Bloomsbury.

Digest of Education Statistics. 2012. National Center for Education Statistics. https://nces.ed.gov/programs/digest/d12/tables/dt12_046.asp

Eberhardt, Jennifer L. 2019. *Biased: Uncovering the Hidden Prejudice that Shapes What We See, Think, and Do*. New York, NY: Penguin Books.

Ehrensaft, Diane. 2016. *The Gender Creative Child: Pathways for Nurturing and Supporting Children Who Live Outside of Gender Boxes*. New York, NY: Experiment Books.

Elliott, K. O. 2016. "Queering Student Perspectives: Gender, Sexuality, and Activism in School." *Sex Education* 16(1):49–62.

Elliot, Shanti. 2015. *Teaching and Learning on the Verge: Democratic Education in Action*. New York: NY. Teachers College Press.

Erickson, Erik H. 1950. *Childhood and Society*. New York, NY: W. W. Norton & Co.

Erikson, Erik H. 1968. *Identity, Youth and Crisis*. New York, NY: W. W. Norton & Co.

Ferfolja, Tania and Lucy Hopkins. 2013. "The Complexities of Workplace Experience for Lesbian and Gay Teachers." *Critical Studies in Education* 54(3):311–324.

Flores, M. A., and C. Day. 2006. "Contexts Which Shape and Reshape New Teachers' Identities: A Multi-Perspective Study." *Teaching and Teacher Education* 22:219–232.

Frame, Oman. 2021. "An Intersection in Our Educational Lives: We Are More than Meets the Eye." Pp. 68–79 in *10 Perspectives on Equity in Education*, edited by Jimmy Casas, Onica L. Mayers, and Jeffrey Zoul. New York, NY: Routledge.

Freud, Sigmund. 1920. *Beyond the Pleasure Principle*. New York, NY: W. W. Norton.

Freire, Paulo. 1968. *Pedagogy of the Oppressed*. New York, NY: The Seabury Press.

Fryer, Roland G. Jr., Devah Pager, and Jorg L. Spenkuch. 2013. "Racial Disparities in Job Finding and Offered Wages." *Journal of Law and Economics* 56(3):633–689.

Garner, Grady L. Jr., and Dennis M. Emano. 2013. "Counseling Lesbian, Gay, Bisexual, Transgender, and Questioning Students." Pp. 189–208 in *Creating Safe and Supportive Learning Environments: A Guide for Working with Lesbian, Gay, Bisexual, Transgender, and Questioning Youth and Families*, edited by E. S. Fisher and K. Komosa-Hawkins. London. Routledge/Taylor & Francis Group.

GenderSpectrum. 2021. www.genderspectrum.org. https://genderspectrum.org/articles/educator-resources

Gilligan, Carol. 1982. *In a Different Voice: Psychological Theory and Women's Development*. Cambridge, MA: Harvard University Press.

GLAAD. 2021. https://www.glaad.org/

GLSEN. 2020. Joseph G. Kosciw. Caitlin M. Clark, Nhan L. Truong. Adrian D. Zongrone. *The 2019 National School Climate Survey*. https://www.glsen.org/research/2019-national-school-climate-survey

GLSEN. 2020. "About Us: Creating a Better World for LGBT Students." https://www.glsen.org/about-us#snt-1

GLSEN. 2021. The GSA Study Report. https://www.glsen.org/gsa-study

Goffman, Erving. 1959. *The Presentation of Self in Everyday Life*. New York, NY: Anchor Books.

Goldberg, Shoshana K. 2021. "Fair Play: The Importance of Sports Participation for Transgender Youth." Center for American Progress. https://www.americanprogress.org/issues/lgbtq-rights/reports/2021/02/08/495502/fair-play/

Good, Catherine, Joshua M. Aronson, and Jayne Ann Harder. 2008. "Problems in the Pipeline: Stereotype Threat and Women's Achievement in High-Level Math Courses." *Journal of Applied Developmental Psychology* 29(1):17–28.

Good, Catherine, Aneeta Rattan, Carol S. Dweck. 2012. "Why Do Women Opt-Out? Sense of Belonging and Women's Representation in Mathematics." *Journal of Personality and Social Psychology* 102(4):700–717.

Guttmacher Institute. www. Guttmacher.org. 2020. https://www.guttmacher.org/fact-sheet/contraceptive-use-among-adolescents-united-states

Guittar, Nicholas. 2014. *Coming Out: The New Dynamics*. Boulder, CO: FirstForum Press.

Heckman, James J. 2008. "Schools, Skills, and Synapses." *Economic Inquiry* 46:289–324.

Herman, Jody. 2013. "Gendered Restrooms and Minority Stress: The Public Regulation of Gender and Its Impact on Transgender People's Lives." *Journal of Public Management & Social Policy* 19(1):65–81.

Hennessy, Terri, and Sara Bloomberg. 2020. "Queering Your Culture: The Importance of Gender Diversity and Inclusion in The Classroom." *Montessori Life: A Publication of the American Montessori Society* 32(1):40–47.

hooks, bell. 1990. *Yearning: Race, Gender, and Cultural Politics*. Boston, MA: South End Press.

hooks, bell. 1994. *Teaching to Transgress: Education as the Practice of Freedom*. New York, NY: Routledge.

Human Rights Campaign. 2021. www.hrc.org.

Illich, Ivan. 1983. *Deschooling Society*. New York, NY: Marion Boyars Publishers.

Imad, Mays. 2020. "Leveraging the Neuroscience of Now." *Inside Higher Ed*. https://www.insidehighered.com/advice/2020/06/03/seven-recommendations-helping-students-thrive-times-trauma

Inclusive STEM Teaching Project. 2022. https://www.inclusivestemteaching.org/

InterAct: Advocates for Intersex Youth. 2020. *FAQ: What Is Intersex?* https://interactadvocates.org/faq/#howcommon

James, Sandy, Jody Herman, Susan Rankin, Mara Keisling, Lisa Mottet, Ma'ayan Anafi. 2016. *The Report of the 2015 U.S. Transgender Survey*. https://transequality.org/sites/default/files/docs/usts/USTS-Full-Report-Dec17.pdf http://hdl.handle.net/20.500.11990/1299

Johnson, Austin H., and Baker A. Rogers. 2020. "'We're the Normal Ones Here': Community Involvement, Peer Support, and Transgender Mental Health." *Sociological Inquiry* 90(1):271–292.

Jones, Jeffrey M. 2021. "LGBT Identification Rises to 5.6% in Latest U.S. Estimate." February 24, 2021. https://news.gallup.com/poll/329708/lgbt-identification-rises-latest-estimate.aspx.

Kar, Sujita Kumar, Ananya Choudhury, and Abhishek Pratap Singh. 2015. "Understanding Normal Development of Adolescent Sexuality: A Bumpy Ride." *Journal of Human Reproductive Sciences* 8(2):70–74.

Katz, Jackson. 2000. *Tough Guise: Violence, Manhood, & American Culture*. Media Education Foundation.

Katz, Jackson. 2013. *Tough Guise 2: Violence, Manhood & American Culture*. Media Education Foundation.

Kendi, Ibram X. 2019. *How to Be an Antiracist*. New York, NY: One World.

Kilbourne, Jean. 2010. https://www.killingussoftly4.org/

Killerman, Sam. 2018. The Genderbread Person, v. 4.

Knipp, Hannah, and Rae Stevenson. 2021. "'A Powerful Visual Statement': Race, Class, and Gender in Uniform and Dress Code Policies in New Orleans Public Charter Schools." *Affilia* 37(1):79–96.

Kosciw, Joseph G., Emily A. Greytak, Adrian D. Zongrone, Caitlin M. Clark, and Nhan L. Truong. 2018. "The 2017 National School Climate Survey: The Experiences of Lesbian, Gay, Bisexual, Transgender, and Queer Youth in Our Nation's Schools." New York, NY: GLSEN. https://www.glsen.org/research/school-climate-survey

Kosciw, Joseph G., Caitlin M. Clark, Nhan L. Truong, and Adrian D. Zongrone. 2020. "The 2019 National School Climate Survey: The Experiences of Lesbian, Gay, Bisexual, Transgender, and Queer Youth in our Nation's Schools." New York, NY: GLSEN. https://www.glsen.org/sites/default/files/2020-10/NSCS-2019-Full-Report_0.pdf

Kralik, Joellen. 2019. "Bathroom Bill" Legislative Tracking. National Conference of State Legislatures. https://www.ncsl.org/research/education/-bathroom-bill-legislative-tracking635951130.aspx

Kroger, Jane. 2007. *Identity Development: Adolescence through Adulthood.* 2nd edition. Thousand Oaks, CA: Sage Publications, Inc.

Lanahan, B. K. 2009. "Teaching about Disasters Reported in the News." In E. Heilman, *Social Studies and Diversity Education: What We Do and Why We Do It.* New York, NY: Teachers College Press p. 243.

Latino, Niki. 2016. "Leadership at the Intersection: A Developmental Framework for Inclusive Leaders." Pp. 25–35 in *Intersectionality in Action: A Guide for Faculty and Campus Leaders for Creating Inclusive Classrooms and Institutions,* edited by Brooke Barnett and Peter Felten. Sterling, VA: Stylus Publishing.

Lewis, Amanda E. 2003. *Race in the Schoolyard: Negotiating the Color Line in Classrooms and Communities.* New Brunswick, NJ: Rutgers University Press.

Lewis, Amanda E., and John B. Diamond. 2015. *Despite the Best Intentions: How Racial Inequality Thrives in Good Schools.* New York, NY: Oxford University Press.

Lopez, Canela. 2021. "More Young People Than Ever Identify as LGBT, and 1 in 4 are Nonbinary." https://www.insider.com/more-lgbt-young-people-identify-nonbinary-2021-7.

Lorber, Judith. 1994. *Paradoxes of Gender.* New Haven, CT: Yale University Press.

Lorber, Judith. 2001. *Gender Inequality: Feminist Theories and Politics.* Los Angeles, CA: Roxbury Pub.

Love, Bettina. 2019. *We Want to do More than Survive: Abolitionist Teaching and the Pursuit of Educational Freedom.* Boston, MA: Beacon Press.

Martin, K. A. 1998. "Becoming a Gendered Body: Practices of Preschools." *American Sociological Review* 63(4):494–511.

Martin, Patricia Yancey. 2004. "Gender as a Social Institution." *Social Forces* 82(4):1249–1273.

Martin, Carol Lynn, and Diane N. Ruble. 2010. "Patterns of Gender Development." *Annual Review of Psychology* 61:353–381.

McAdoo, Phillip. 2019. *Independent Queers: LGBTQ Educators in Independant Schools Speak Out*. Herdon, VA: Mascot Books.

McLanahan, S., and C. Percheski. 2008. "Family Structure and the Reproduction of Inequalities." *Annual Review of Sociology* 34:257–276.

Messner, Michael A. 2000. "Barbie Girls versus Sea Monsters: Children Constructing Gender." *Gender & Society* 14:765–784.

Messner, Michael A. 2002. *Taking the Field: Women, Men, and Sports*. NED-New edition, Vol. 4. Minneapolis: University of Minnesota Press.

MissRepresentation.org. 2021. http://therepresentationproject.org/film/miss-representation-film/

Molotch, Harvey, and Laura Noren. 2010. *Toilet: Public Restrooms and the Politics of Sharing*. New York, NY: New York University Press.

Morris, Edward. 2012. *Learning the Hard Way: Masculinity, Place, and the Gender Gap in Education*. New Brunswick, NJ: Rutgers University Press.

Morris, Monique W. 2015. *Pushout: The Criminalization of Black Girls in Schools*. New York, NY: The New Press.

Nath, R., M. Ybarra, M. MacAulay, K. Oppenheim, L. Jackson, I. F. Strøm, R. Sullivan, S. Millar, and E. Saewyc. 2021. "Comparing Factors Shaping Sexual Violence Perpetration for Sexual and Gender Minority Youth and Cisgender Heterosexual Youth." *Journal of Interpersonal Violence*.

National Center for Transgender Equality. 2016. "Fact Sheet on U. S. Department of Education Policy on Transgender Students." https://transequality.org/sites/default/files/ED-DCL-Fact-Sheet.pdf

National Coalition for Women and Girls in Education (NCWGE). 2017. *Title IX at 45: Advancing Opportunity through Equity in Education*. Washington, DC. https://www.ncwge.org/TitleIX45/Title%20IX%20at%2045-Advancing%20Opportunity%20through%20Equity%20in%20Education.pdf

Newsom, Jennifer Siebel. 2011. *Miss Representation*. Roco Films Educational

Newsom, Jennifer Siebel. 2015. *The Mask You Live in*. The Representation Project

Nicolazzo, Z. 2017. *Trans* in College: Transgender Students Strategies for Navigating Campus Life and the Institutional Politics of Inclusion.* Sterling, VA: Stylus Publishing.

Nishioka, V., M. Coe, A. Burke, M. Hanita, and J. Sprague. 2011. "Student-Reported Overt and Relational Aggression and Victimization in Grades 3–8." *Issues and Answers Report, REL* 114:1–42.

Olsen, Brad. 2008. "Teacher Identity as a Useful Frame for Study and Practice of Teacher Education." *Teacher Education Quarterly* 35(3):3–6.

Olsen, Kristen. 2014. "Telling Our Stories: Narrative and Framing in the Movement for Same-Sex Marriage." *Social Movement Studies* 13(2):248–266.

Olson, K. R., A. C. Key, and N. R. Eaton. 2015. "Gender Cognition in Transgender Children." *Psychological Science* 26(4):467–474.

Orenstein, Peggy. 2011. *Cinderella Ate My Daughter: Dispatches From the Front Lines of the New Girlie-Girl Culture.* New York, NY: HarperCollins Publishers.

Orenstein, Peggy. 2016. *Girls & Sex: Navigating the Complicated New Landscape.* New York, NY: HarperCollins Publishers.

Ortiz, Anna. M., and Lori D. Patton. 2012. "Awareness of Self." PP. 9–16 in *Why Aren't We There Yet? Taking Personal Responsibility for Creating an Inclusive Campus*, edited by Arminio, J., Torres, V., and Pope, L. R. Sterling, VA: Stylus Publishing.

Osterweil, Neil. 2007. "APA: Simple Screen Improves Suicide Risk Assessment." https://www.medpagetoday.org/meetingcoverage/apa/5770?vpass=1

Pascoe, C. J. 2007. *Dude, You're a Fag: Masculinity and Sexuality in High School.* University of California Press.

Pascoe, C. J., and Tristan Bridges. 2016. *Exploring Masculinities: Identity, Inequality, Continuity and Change.* Thousand Oaks, CA: Oxford Press.

Pastel, Encian, Katie Steele, Julie Nicholson, Cyndi Maurer, Julia Hennock, Johnathan Julian, Tess Unger, and Nathanael Flynn. 2019. *Supporting Gender Diversity in Early Childhood Education: A Practical Guide.* Philadelphia, PA: Jessica Kingsley Publishers.

Petri, A. E., and A. Das. 2021. "The U.S. Women's Soccer Team Files an Opening Brief in Their Ongoing Equal Pay Lawsuit." *New York*

Times. https://www.nytimes.com/2021/07/24/sports/olympics/us-womens-soccer-equal-pay-lawsuit.html?.?mc=aud_dev&ad-keywords=auddevgate&gclid=Cj0KCQjwg7KJBhDyARIsAHrAXaHVGwtHLe-XDxvQXUE3g1JW2rCSrb1vtyNIG1tIKCdYXMpRpneqJcQaAtCkEALw_wcB&gclsrc=aw.ds

Pew Research Center. 2018. "Stay-at-Home Moms and Dads Account for About One-in-Five U.S. Parents." https://www.pewresearch.org/fact-tank/2018/09/24/stay-at-home-moms-and-dads-account-for-about-one-in-five-u-s-parents/

PFLAG. 2021. "Cultivating Respect: Safe Schools for All." https://pflag.org/cultivating-respect-safe-schools-all

Piaget, Jean. 1972. Play and Development (A Symposium with contributions by Jean Piaget, Peter H. Wolff, René A. Spitz, Konrad Lorenz, Lois Barclay Murphy and Erik H. Erickson), edited by Maria W. Piers. New York, NY: W. W. Norton & Company.

Picho, K., A. Rodriguez, and L. Finnie. 2013. "Exploring the Moderating Role of Context on the Mathematics Performance of Females under Stereotype Threat: A Meta-Analysis." *The Journal of Social Psychology* 153:299–333.

Planned Parenthood. 2021. "What's Intersex?" Retrieved https://www.plannedparenthood.org/learn/gender-identity/sex-gender-identity/whats-intersex.

Porter, Tony. 2010. "A Call to Men." https://www.ted.com/talks/tony_porter_a_call_to_men

Putnam, Robert D. 2015. *Our Kids: The American Dream in Crisis*. New York, NY: Simon & Schuster.

Rafalovich, Adam. 2005. "Relational Troubles and Semi Official Suspicion: Educators and the Medicalization of "Unruly" Children." *Symbolic Interaction* 28(1). https://doi.org/10.1525/si.2005.28.1.25

Ray, Brett. 2015. *My Name Is Brett: Truths from a Trans Christian*. Denmark: CreateSpace Independent Publishing Platform.

Ritch, Savin Williams. 2006. *The New Gay Teenager*. Boston, MA: Harvard University Press.

Ritch, Savin Williams. 2016. *Becoming Who I Am: Young Men on Being Gay*. Boston, MA: Harvard University Press.

Ridgway, C. and C. Healy. 1997. "Evaluation of Empowerment in a High School Geometry Class." *The Mathematics Teacher* 90(9):738–741.

Rios, Victor. 2017. *Human Targets: Schools, Police, and the Criminalization of Latino Youth*. Chicago, IL: University of Chicago Press.

Risman, Barbara J. 1998. *Gender Vertigo: American Families in Transition*. New Haven, CT: Yale University Press.

Rodgers and Scott, 2008. "The Development of the Personal Self and Professional Identity in Learning to Teach". Pp. 733–757 in *Handbook of Research on Teacher Education*, edited by D. J. Clandinin and J. Husu. California: Sage Publications.

Rogers, Baker A. 2020. *Trans Men in the South: Becoming Men*. Lanham, MD: Lexington Books.

Russell, Stephen, Katerina Sinclair, V. Paul Poteat, and Brian Koenig. 2012. "Adolescent Health and Harassment Based on Discriminatory Bias". *American Journal Public Health* 102:493–495.

Sachs, J. 2005. "Teacher Education and the Development of Professional Identity: Learning to be a Teacher." Pp. 5–21 in *Connecting Policy and Practice: Challenges for Teaching and Learning in Schools and Universities*, edited by P. M. Denicolo, and M. Kompf. Routledge, Taylor and Francis Group.

Sadker, Myra, and David Sadker. 1994. "The Miseducation of Boys: Changing the Script." Pp. 42–76 in *Failing at Fairness: How America's Schools Cheat Girls*, edited by Myra Sadker and David Sadker. New York, NY: Scibner.

The SafeZone Initiative. 2021. https://www.theszinitiative.org/

Schor, Juliet. 1991. *The Overworked American: The Unexpected Decline of Leisure*. Basic Books.

Schwalbe, Michael. 2014. *Rigging the Game: How Inequality Is Reproduced in Everyday Life*. Oxford: Oxford University Press.

Spade, Dean. 2018. "We Still Need Pronoun Go-Rounds." http://www.deanspade.net/2018/12/01/we-still-need-pronoun-go-rounds/.

Sprague, Jeffrey, Vicki Nishioka, and Stephen G. Smith. 2012. "Safe Schools, Positive Behavior Supports, and Mental Health Supports: Lessons Learned from Three Safe Schools/Healthy Students Communities." *Journal of School Violence* 6(2):93–115.

Steele, Dorothy M., and Becki Cohn-Vargas. 2013. *Identity Safe Classrooms: Places to Belong and Learn*. California: Corwin Press.

Stringer, Jac. 2011. "All About Pronouns." https://jenniferrickardmft.com/wp-content/uploads/2017/04/Pronouns-Handout-copy.pdf

Sturrock, John. (ed.). 1979. *Structuralism and Since: From Levi-Strauss to Derrida*. Oxford: Oxford University Press,

Sue, Derald Wing. 2010. "Microaggressions, Marginality, and Oppression: An Introduction." Pp. 3–22 in *Microaggressions and Marginality: Manifestation, Dynamics, and Impact*, edited by S. D. Wing. Hoboken, NJ: John Wiley & Sons, Inc.

Tatum, Beverly Daniel 1997. *"Why Are All the Black Kids Sitting Together in the Cafeteria?" and Other Conversations about Race*. New York, NY: Basic Books.

Thompson, Elizabeth. 2021. "In HB2's Shadow, Advocates Fear the Consequences of Anti-trans Bills in NC." https://www.northcarolinahealthnews.org/2021/09/15/in-hb2s-shadow-advocates-fear-the-consequences-of-anti-trans-bills-in-nc/

Thompson, Martha E., and Michael Armato. 2012. *Investigating Gender: Developing a Feminist Sociological Imagination*. Malden, MA: Polity Press.

Toomey, R. and Caitlyn Ryan. 2010. "Gender Non-conforming Lesbian, Gay, Bisexual, and Transgender Youth: School Victimization and Young Adult Psychosocial Adjustment." *Psychology of Sexual Orientation and Gender Diversity* 1(S):71–80. doi:10.1037/2329–0382.1.S.71

Travers, Ann. 2018. *The Trans Generation: How Trans Kids (and Their Parents) Are Creating a Gender Revolution*. New York, NY: New York University Press.

The Trevor Project. 2020. "2020 National Survey on LGBTQ Youth Mental Health." https://www.thetrevorproject.org/survey-2020/?section=Introduction

The Trevor Project. 2020a. *Research Brief: LGBTQ Youth Sports Participation*. The Trevor Project. West Hollywood, CA. https://www.thetrevorproject.org/2020/06/23/research-brief-lgbtq-youth-sports-participation/.

The Trevor Project. 2021. "National Survey on LGBTQ Youth Mental Health." https://www.thetrevorproject.org/survey-2021/

The Trevor Project. 2021. "Sexual Orientation: It Is Just One Piece of Who You Are." https://www.thetrevorproject.org/resources/category/sexual-orientation/

Veen, Klaas, Peter Sleegers, and Piet-Hein Ven. 2005. "One Teacher's Identity, Emotions, and Commitment to Change: A Case Study into the Cognitive–Affective Processes of a Secondary School Teacher in the Context of Reforms." *Teaching and Teacher Education* 21:917–934.

Wade, Lisa, and Myra Marx Ferree. 2015. 2019. *Gender: Ideas, Interactions, Institutions*. New York, NY: Norton Publishing.

Watkins, Paul, and Edward Mereno. 2017. "Bathrooms without Borders: Transgender Students Argue Separate Is not Equal". *The Clearing House: A Journal of Educational Strategies, Issues and Ideas* 90(5–6):166–171.

Wernick, L. J., A. Kulick, and M. Chin. 2017. "Gender Identity Disparities in Bathroom Safety and Wellbeing among High School Students." *Journal of Youth and Adolescence* 46:917–930.

West, Candace, and Don H. Zimmerman. 1987. "Doing Gender." *Gender & Society* 1(2):125–151.

West, Candace, and Don H. Zimmerman. 2009. "Accounting for Doing Gender." *Gender & Society* 23(1):112–122.

White House: Executive Order on Preventing and Combating Discrimination on the Basis of Gender Identity or Sexual Orientation 2021. The White House. https://www.whitehouse.gov/briefing-room/presidential-actions/2021/01/20/executive-order-preventing-and-combating-discrimination-on-basis-of-gender-identity-or-sexual-orientation/

Williams, Ritch Savin. 2017. *Mostly Straight: Sexual Fluidity among Men*. Boston, MA: Harvard University Press.

Williams Institute at UCLA. https://williamsinstitute.law.ucla.edu/

Williams, Trash, Jennifer Connolly, Debra Pepler, and Wendy Craig. 2005. "Peer Victimization, Social Support, and Psychosocial Adjustment of Sexual Minority Adolescents." *Journal of Youth and Adolescence* 34(5):471–482. doi:10.1007/s10964-005-7264-x

Wickliffe, J. 2019. "Answering the 'Million Dollar' Question: The Meaning of 'Sex' for the Purposes of Title IX, Title VII, and the Equal Protection Clause, and Its Impact on Transgender Students' Membership in Fraternal Organizations." *University of Arkansas at Little Rock Law Review* 42: 327.

Wink, Joan. 2011. *Critical Pedagogy: Notes from the Real World*, 4th Edition. New York, NY: Pearson.

Wiseman, Rosalind. 2016. *Owning up: Empowering Adolescents to Confront Social Cruelty, Bullying, and Injustice.* Corwin Press.

Wood, M. A., W. M. Bukowski, and E. Lis. 2016. "The Digital Self: How Social Media Serves as a Setting that Shapes Youth's Emotional Experiences." *Adolescent Research Review* 1:163–173.

Wortham, Sue C. 2006. *Early Childhood Curriculum: Developmental Bases for Learning and Teaching*. Edisi ke-4. Upper Saddle River, NJ: Pearson Merrill Prentice Hall.

Xu Guifieng, Strathearn L., B. Liu, B. Yang, and W. Bao. 2018. "Twenty-Year Trends in Diagnosed Attention-Deficit/Hyperactivity Disorder Among US Children and Adolescents, 1997–2016." *Journal of Adolescent Medicine* 1(4):e181471.

Yunger, J. L., P. R. Carver, and D. G. Perry. 2004. "Does Gender Identity Influence Children's Psychological Well-Being?" *Developmental Psychology* 40(4):572–582. https://doi.org/10.1037/0012-1649.40.4.572

Zembylas, Michalinos. 2003. "Emotions and Teacher Identity: A Poststructural Perspective." *Teachers and Teaching* 9(3):213–238.